INTERNATIONAL DEVELOPMENT IN FOCUS

# What Matters for Learning in Malawi?

Evidence from the Malawi Longitudinal School Survey

SALMAN ASIM AND RAVINDER CASLEY GERA

© 2024 International Bank for Reconstruction and Development / The World Bank
1818 H Street NW, Washington, DC 20433
Telephone: 202-473-1000; Internet: www.worldbank.org

Some rights reserved

1 2 3 4   27 26 25 24

Books in this series are published to communicate the results of World Bank research, analysis, and operational experience with the least possible delay. The extent of language editing varies from book to book.

This work is a product of the staff of The World Bank with external contributions. The findings, interpretations, and conclusions expressed in this work do not necessarily reflect the views of The World Bank, its Board of Executive Directors, or the governments they represent. The World Bank does not guarantee the accuracy, completeness, or currency of the data included in this work and does not assume responsibility for any errors, omissions, or discrepancies in the information, or liability with respect to the use of or failure to use the information, methods, processes, or conclusions set forth. The boundaries, colors, denominations, and other information shown on any map in this work do not imply any judgment on the part of The World Bank concerning the legal status of any territory or the endorsement or acceptance of such boundaries.

Nothing herein shall constitute or be construed or considered to be a limitation upon or waiver of the privileges and immunities of The World Bank, all of which are specifically reserved.

**Rights and Permissions**

This work is available under the Creative Commons Attribution 3.0 IGO license (CC BY 3.0 IGO) http://creativecommons.org/licenses/by/3.0/igo. Under the Creative Commons Attribution license, you are free to copy, distribute, transmit, and adapt this work, including for commercial purposes, under the following conditions:

**Attribution**—Please cite the work as follows: Asim, Salman, and Ravinder Casley Gera. 2024. *What Matters for Learning in Malawi? Evidence from the Malawi Longitudinal School Survey*. International Development in Focus. Washington, DC: World Bank. doi:10.1596/978-1-4648-2052-6. License: Creative Commons Attribution CC BY 3.0 IGO

**Translations**—If you create a translation of this work, please add the following disclaimer along with the attribution: *This translation was not created by The World Bank and should not be considered an official World Bank translation. The World Bank shall not be liable for any content or error in this translation.*

**Adaptations**—If you create an adaptation of this work, please add the following disclaimer along with the attribution: *This is an adaptation of an original work by The World Bank. Views and opinions expressed in the adaptation are the sole responsibility of the author or authors of the adaptation and are not endorsed by The World Bank.*

**Third-party content**—The World Bank does not necessarily own each component of the content contained within the work. The World Bank therefore does not warrant that the use of any third-party-owned individual component or part contained in the work will not infringe on the rights of those third parties. The risk of claims resulting from such infringement rests solely with you. If you wish to re-use a component of the work, it is your responsibility to determine whether permission is needed for that re-use and to obtain permission from the copyright owner. Examples of components can include, but are not limited to, tables, figures, or images.

All queries on rights and licenses should be addressed to World Bank Publications, The World Bank, 1818 H Street NW, Washington, DC 20433, USA; e-mail: pubrights@worldbank.org.

ISBN: 978-1-4648-2052-6
DOI: 10.1596/978-1-4648-2052-6

Cover illustration: © World Bank; permission required for reuse. Cover image by Lerato Honde.
Cover design: Debra Naylor / Naylor Design Inc.

# Contents

*Acknowledgments*   *vii*
*About the Authors*   *ix*
*Executive Summary*   *xi*
*Abbreviations*   *xvii*

**Introduction: Why Has Malawi Performed Poorly in Education?**   **1**

Key points   1
Low learning levels despite expanded school access   1
Insufficient, inadequately targeted financing and weak data systems   2
Persistence of significant inequities in learning outcomes between schools   5
Insights for new policy directions from the Malawi Longitudinal School Survey   5
Notes   11
References   11

CHAPTER 1: **Malawi's Low-Level Education Equilibrium**   **13**

Key points   13
Low service standards and high student absenteeism in primary schools   13
Persistence of high repetition and dropout rates   15
Low learning achievement   16
Persistence of inequitable outcomes between and within schools   17
Conclusions: Challenging Malawi's low-level education equilibrium   19
Annex 1A: Summary statistics on learning outcome disparities   19
Notes   20
References   21

CHAPTER 2: **Schools: Learning Disadvantages in Remote Schools**   **23**

Key points   23
Constraints in learning conditions at the typical school   23
Inequities in conditions between remote schools and those near trading centers   24
Poorer student outcomes at remote schools than at those near trading centers   27

What matters for learning?    28
Conclusions: Inequities in school conditions and learning based on location    29
Annex 2A: Statistical and regression tables    30
Notes    36
References    37

**CHAPTER 3: Teachers: Learning Constraints from Large Class Sizes    39**

Key points    39
Poor distribution of teachers between grades    39
Teacher absence and inadequate teaching time    41
Adaptation of teaching strategies for large class sizes    41
What matters for learning?    43
Conclusions: Inequities in schools' teacher distribution, management, and performance    45
Annex 3A: Statistical and regression tables    45
Notes    50
References    51

**CHAPTER 4: Students: The Importance of Home Background and Support    53**

Key points    53
Diversity of Malawi's student population    53
What matters for learning?    54
Conclusions: School-level population differences, particularly in mindset, matter for learning    57
Annex 4A: Summary statistics    58
Notes    58
References    59

**CHAPTER 5: Focus on Girls' Learning    61**

Key points    61
Student-level inequities: The main source of outcome disparities    61
Female students are left behind in Malawi's primary schools    62
What matters for girls' learning?    64
Conclusions: Contributions of individual student characteristics, particularly gender, to inequities in learning outcomes    66
Annex 5A: Regression analyses    67
Notes    69
References    70

**CHAPTER 6: The Effect of Multiple Disadvantages on Student Achievement    71**

Key points    71
Introducing the Disadvantage Index    71
Profound impact of multiple disadvantages on learning outcomes    73
How targeted investments in the neediest schools can improve learning    73
Conclusions: Raising learning outcomes by targeting resources to disadvantaged schools    75
Annex 6A: Statistical and regression tables    76
Notes    78
References    79

**Conclusion: The Challenge and Opportunity of Longitudinal Education Data**   81

Summary of findings from baseline data   81
Data-driven reforms, investments, and analyses   81
Outlook for longitudinal data-driven policy making in low-income countries   82
Notes   83
References   83

Appendix A   **Data and Methodology**   85

## Boxes

I.1   Malawi Education Reform Program   4
I.2   The MLSS as longitudinal survey   7
I.3   The MLSS learning assessments and knowledge scores   10
2.1   Inequitable teacher distribution between remote schools and schools near trading centers   25
3.1   Teachers' perspectives on large class sizes   43
4.1   Inequities in student populations between remote schools and those close to trading centers   55
4.2   A sample of students' attitudes toward their schools and learning   57
5.1   Influence of personal characteristics on student-level outcomes   62
6.1   The Disadvantage Index   72

## Figures

ES.1   Average learning outcomes at rural primary schools, by number of disadvantages, 2016   xv
I.1   The administrative data lens versus the MLSS data lens   8
1.1   Ratios of pupils to classrooms, teachers, and latrines in primary schools, 2016   14
1.2   Effects of dropout and repetition rates on students' progression to higher grades   15
1.3   Share of students who can perform basic mathematics and English tasks by end of grade 4, 2016   16
1.4   Shares of grade 4 students who correctly complete tasks, by subject and grade-level curriculum, 2016   17
1.5   Variance of student outcomes between highest- and lowest-performing primary schools, 2016   18
1.6   Variance of student knowledge scores, by subject, 2016   18
2.1   Comparison of infrastructure and materials in remote schools versus those near TCs, 2016   24
2.2   Comparison of SIG investments in remote schools versus those near TCs, by category, 2016   27
2.3   Dropout rates in remote schools versus those near TCs, by grade, 2016   27
2.4   Knowledge scores, by distance from TC, 2016   28
3.1   Average PTR, by grade, 2016   40
3.2   Shares of primary school teachers using selected practices, Malawi and other Sub-Saharan African countries, 2016   42
B4.1.1   Shares of Malawian students with selected household characteristics in remote schools versus those close to a trading center, 2016   55
5.1   Distribution of knowledge scores, by gender, 2016   63
5.2   Primary school dropout rates and PSLCE outcomes, by gender   64
6.1   School conditions included in the Disadvantage Index   72
6.2   Average knowledge scores at primary schools, by number of disadvantages, 2016   73
6.3   Estimated knowledge scores in overcrowded schools where PqTR is reduced   75

## Map

I.1　Malawian primary schools included in the MLSS baseline sample, 2016　9

## Tables

ES.1　Contrast in average knowledge scores, by student characteristics, 2016　xiv
I.1　Comparison of conditions and learning outcomes in two schools within the same zone　6
1A.1　Performance indicators of student participation and learning outcomes in rural primary schools, 2016　19
2A.1　Summary statistics on grade 1–8 school conditions and facilities, 2016　30
2A.2　Summary statistics on school finances and expenditures, 2016　31
2A.3　Regression analysis of school-level factors' impacts on grade 4 learning outcomes　32
3.1　Correlation of achievement gaps with teacher characteristics and practices, 2016　44
3A.1　Summary statistics on teacher characteristics　45
3A.2　Summary statistics of teacher practices in lessons observed　46
3A.3　Regression analysis of impact of teacher practices and characteristics on student knowledge scores, 2016　47
4.1　Effects on achievement gaps in Malawian schools' student populations, by indicator, 2016　56
4A.1　Summary statistics on student characteristics, 2016　58
5.1　Decomposition of variance in test scores　62
5.2　Contrast in knowledge scores, by student characteristic, 2016　63
5A.1　Impact of school-level factors on female students' school-level learning　67
5A.2　Differential impact on learning of student gender, school-level factors, and cross-level interactions　68
6A.1　Distribution of school disadvantage conditions　76
6A.2　Regression estimates on key outcome indicators, by Disadvantage Index　77
6A.3　Knowledge score impact of PqTR reduction　78

# Acknowledgments

We thank the Ministry of Education of Malawi, in particular Honorable Minister Madalitso Wirima Kambauwa, Secretary of Education Mangani Chilala Katundu, Director of Basic Education Grace Milner, Deputy Director of Education Planning–Policy and Budget Edwin Kanyoma, and Deputy Director for Education Management Information System and Monitoring and Evaluation James Namfuko; former Directors of Education Planning Rodwell Mzonde and Francis Zhuwao; and former Directors of Basic Education Joseph Chimombo and Gossam Mafuta, for support in collection of independent data on a nationally representative sample of public primary schools.

Aneesa Arur, Sajitha Bashir, Flora Kelmendi, Safaa El-Kogali, Tobias Linden, Muna Salih Meky, Innocent Mulindwa, Hugh Riddell, Greg Toulmin, Inam Ul Haq, Quentin Wodon, and other World Bank colleagues in Malawi and elsewhere provided much encouragement, support, and advice. Martin Moreno, Xu Wang, and Laura White provided substantive comments and edits, and Gift Banda, Johannes Brehm, Chris Burningham, Dmitry Chugunov, Radhika Kapoor, Linda Matumbi, Leah Mziya, Stefan Nippes, and Siddharth Ramalingam gave invaluable research assistance. We also thank Her Excellency Ingrid Marie Mikelsen, Vigdis Aaslund Cristofoli, Miriam Nandi, and Elin Ruud, Royal Norwegian Embassy; and Sabina Morley and Arianna Zanolini, UK Foreign, Commonwealth and Development Office, for comments and suggestions and for funding the preparation of this report.

The findings, interpretations, and conclusions expressed herein are our own and do not necessarily represent the views of the World Bank, its board of directors, or any of its member countries. All remaining errors are our own.

# About the Authors

**Salman Asim** is a senior economist in the Education Global Practice at the World Bank, currently leading the World Bank's engagement on technology and innovation in K-12 education, adult learning systems for 21st-century skills, and labor market transitions in response to green technologies and automation (artificial intelligence/digital) for education programs in China, the Republic of Korea, and Mongolia. Previously, he led the World Bank's operations on systemwide basic education reforms in Ethiopia and Malawi, delivering US$250 million in International Development Association and Global Partnership for Education investments in these countries. He further co-led the design and implementation for the Education Program for Results (US$200 million) and led analytical products in Tanzania. He has also worked on education programs in South Asia and on several impact evaluations in the Development Economics Research Group. He has published in peer-reviewed journals. Asim recently led the large-scale Malawi Longitudinal School Survey with US$5 million in external research grants. His work in Malawi won the Joyce Cain Award for Distinguished Research on People of African Descent from the Comparative and International Education Society. Asim is a Rhodes Scholar and holds an M.Phil. in economics from the University of Oxford.

**Ravinder Casley Gera** is an education specialist at the World Bank focusing on education finance, impact evaluation, and the determinants of foundational learning. Gera believes that every child around the world deserves a high-quality education and is passionate about addressing the constraints that can prevent children from learning and achieving their potential. He has played a leadership role in a wide range of research, overseeing data collection and analysis for the Malawi Longitudinal School Survey over five years and mutiple rounds and evaluation outputs. He has prepared more than US$400 million in investment projects for the World Bank in Ethiopia, Malawi, and Tanzania. Originally from the United Kingdom, Casley Gera was a Kennedy Scholar at the Graduate School of Arts and Sciences at Harvard University and holds an MSc in development studies from the London School of Economics and Political Science.

# Executive Summary

## INTRODUCTION

**Without adequate financing and targeting, Malawi has struggled to meet ambitious policy goals and equitably provide quality education to its school-age population.** Since the introduction of free primary education in 1994, Malawi has experienced rapid increases in enrollment rates, which have outstripped the increase in resources and capacity to deliver learning. Education sector reforms have often set ambitious policy goals without the financing and targeting needed to have an impact. The result is a status quo of schooling with poor learning outcomes and wide learning disparities both between and within schools.

**The Malawi Longitudinal School Survey (MLSS), launched in 2016, was intended to create a robust, representative, and independent measurement system—the first of its kind in Africa—to dynamically track performance of the Malawian education system, anchored to education sector reforms spearheaded by the government.**[1] Malawi's education system faced challenges in data quality, reliability, and use, frustrating attempts to target resources to reduce inequities. In response to these challenges, the Malawi Ministry of Education—in partnership with the World Bank and supported by research grants from the Royal Norwegian Embassy and the United Kingdom's Foreign, Commonwealth and Development Office—developed the MLSS, a nationally representative survey of schools, teachers, and students in Malawi. The MLSS collects data on a wide range of indicators and, at baseline, tested more than 13,000 grade 4 students across both rural and urban schools in all districts of Malawi.[2]

**This report summarizes the findings of the MLSS baseline and presents the most detailed picture ever published of conditions, practices, and outcomes in Malawi's primary schools.** Forthcoming analyses and evaluations informed by the subsequent rounds of the MLSS will measure the impact of promising recent interventions with potential to target resources more effectively and raise learning outcomes.[3]

**The MLSS baseline data depict high student absence, grade repetition, and dropout rates as well as poor learning outcomes.** Learning infrastructure is generally of poor quality, and classes are plagued by overcrowding, which is worsened by high repetition rates. As a result, Malawian communities have reduced their demand for education (as demonstrated by high absence and dropout rates). Furthermore, learning levels in general are low: students who advance to grade 4 struggle with items aligned with even the grade 1–2 curricula, and about 15 percent of grade 4 students have learned almost nothing (as discussed in chapter 1). These poor learning outcomes have been severely exacerbated by the COVID-19 pandemic and the associated closure of schools.

**Moreover, education outcomes are highly variable, producing inequities both between and within schools.** Although the overall performance of the education system is poor, the MLSS also shows significant variation in absence, repetition, dropout, and learning outcomes both between and within schools, driven by inequities in conditions (as discussed in chapter 2). Schools in remote areas achieve the lowest learning outcomes and face the most severe challenges in terms of school infrastructure, teaching and learning materials, and staffing. At the same time, learning outcomes within a single class vary considerably, effectively creating multigrade classes, with girls, minority-language students, students without literate parents, and those without a pre-primary education achieving lower learning outcomes. These low and inequitable learning outcomes mean that Malawi performs poorly on the World Bank's Human Capital Index (World Bank 2021).

Based on the descriptive analysis of the first-round MLSS, the report makes several recommendations to equitably improve foundational learning in lower-primary grades.

## RECOMMENDATIONS TO ADDRESS INEQUITIES BY TARGETING RESOURCES TO THE NEEDIEST SCHOOLS AND STUDENTS

### Target resources to meet the needs of remote schools

**The MLSS data show that students attending schools in remote areas drop out more frequently, and achieve lower learning outcomes, than those in schools close to *trading centers*—that is, commercial hubs.**[4] Typical test performance for a grade 4 student in English, mathematics, and Chichewa drops consistently for every additional kilometer from their school to the nearest trading center; dropout rates also increase (refer to chapter 2). These disparities in test scores reflect large differences in conditions between schools: remote schools are more likely to lack basic teaching and learning materials, experience more delays in receipt of school grants, and are more likely to spend grants on teacher housing and community teachers rather than on student learning materials and teaching aids—factors associated with high test scores.

**Improving the targeting of resources will address inequities and enable remote schools to make investments that have a stronger impact on test scores.** The reforms to school grants supported by the Malawi Education Reform Program (discussed in box I.1 in the introduction to this report) are an important step in aligning financing of schools with need.

### Improve teacher distribution between remote schools and schools close to trading centers

**Extreme variations in staffing exacerbate poor learning environments in remote schools.** Remote schools are much more likely to have pupil-teacher ratios above 90 to 1, to rely heavily on junior teachers, and to have no female teachers (as discussed in chapter 2). Recent improvements in districts' allocations of teachers to schools must be expanded upon to ensure that all districts close the pupil-teacher ratio gaps between schools. The revamped hardship support scheme for teachers in remote schools (discussed in box I.1) is a vital step to retain competent teachers in remote schools, as are the district-level action plans to support female teachers to accept more remote postings.

### Reduce large class sizes to enable teachers to teach effectively

**When in the classroom, Malawi's primary school teachers are as likely as those in comparable countries to exhibit many positive teaching practices.** However, they are much less likely to set and mark homework and are not generally available to students for questions after class (as discussed in chapter 3). This behavior is in part a response to large class sizes. In addition to improving teacher distribution between remote schools and those close to trading centers, improving teacher distribution *within* schools to rationalize class sizes in lower grades could improve teaching and learning. Extensive construction of additional classrooms is required in many schools to support this rationalization of class sizes. Furthermore, official systems of supervision need to be strengthened, particularly in remote areas, to support teachers in ways that enhance morale and effort.

### Improve access to pre-primary education

**Pre-primary education does not reach all students in Malawi: only 62 percent of students in the MLSS baseline sample had attended a year or more.** However, schools with a larger share of students with pre-primary education achieve significantly higher test scores than those with a lower share (as discussed in chapter 4). Investment in improved pre-primary access is required to ensure that all students can benefit from the boost in foundational learning that pre-primary education can provide. In the short term, increasing support to schools with low shares of students with a pre-primary background so that those schools can offer remedial activities—such as the support provided by the recent reforms to school grants (discussed in box I.1)—may be a promising low-cost way to raise learning levels.

### Foster inclusive school cultures, and increase support for girls

**The MLSS data demonstrate that gender inequities in learning in Malawi not only are large but also emerge at an early stage.** At the student level, gender has the largest impact on grade 4 learning outcomes—with female students, on average, performing worse than boys (refer to table ES.1).

TABLE ES.1 **Contrast in average knowledge scores, by student characteristics, 2016**

| CHARACTERISTIC | AVERAGE KNOWLEDGE SCORE | |
|---|---|---|
| Gender | Girls<br>494 | Boys<br>513 |
| Repetition of grade | Repeaters<br>506 | Nonrepeaters<br>512 |
| Absenteeism | Absent last week<br>494 | Present last week<br>507 |
| Grade-appropriate age | Over-age (>14 years)<br>499 | Appropriate age (11 years)<br>507 |
| Parental literacy | Illiterate parents<br>499 | Literate parents<br>504 |
| Language | Minority-language-speaking<br>499 | Chichewa-speaking<br>505 |

*Source:* Malawi Longitudinal School Survey baseline (2016) data, World Bank.
*Note:* The table compares the predicted value of the overall knowledge score for contrasting groups of students in rural schools. These predicted values are estimated from hierarchical linear regression model after controlling for student, teacher, and school characteristics. To create the knowledge scores, grade 4 students are tested in English, mathematics, and Chichewa. Scores are adapted to a mean-centered scale centered at 500 using item response theory. Subject scores are averaged to produce student overall score. For more detail, see the Introduction.

The difference in average test performance between girls and boys in grade 4 is equivalent to about four months' learning. Interventions to tackle girls' high dropout rates in upper grades may have only limited potential because girls are already lagging in learning by the time they reach these grades. Interviews with school leaders whose female student populations perform better than predicted by multivariate regressions suggest that school, head teacher, and community support can reduce learning inequities between boys and girls (as discussed in chapter 5).

**We recommend focusing on training teachers and school leaders to build school cultures that are inclusive of all students and increasing community support for girls.** For example, the "learner mentors" program (discussed in box I.1), in which female secondary students act as mentors for female primary students, is a promising step forward.

### Use the Disadvantage Index to identify the neediest schools

**We develop a Disadvantage Index to capture key aspects of school conditions, staffing, and student populations that negatively affect learning.** Across subjects, learning outcomes are lower in schools with a greater number of disadvantages (refer to figure ES.1). It is necessary to use a data-driven approach to transition Malawi's education system into one that carefully targets resources to the neediest schools. The Disadvantage Index provides a powerful targeting tool to underpin education investments in the sector.

#### FIGURE ES.1
**Average learning outcomes at rural primary schools, by number of disadvantages, 2016**

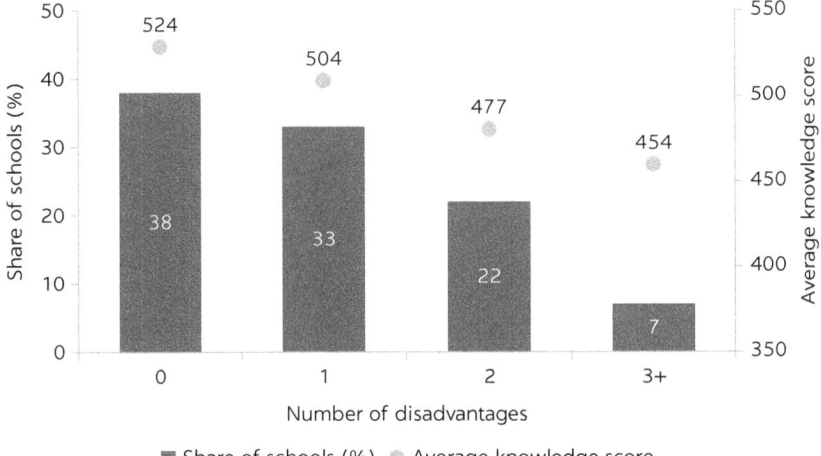

*Source:* Malawi Longitudinal School Survey baseline (2016) data, World Bank.
*Note:* N = 509. The Disadvantage Index includes the following disadvantages: School is more than 10 kilometers from the nearest trading center. School meets three or four shortage conditions for student learning materials (SLM). School has no women among the head teacher; deputy head teacher; infant, junior, and senior section heads; School Management Committee chair and vice chair; or parent-teacher association chair and vice chair. School has both a pupil-teacher ratio and pupil-classroom ratio above 90 to 1. Fewer than 30 percent of school's students have one or more year of pre-primary education. For a detailed explanation of SLM shortage conditions, see chapter 6, table 6.1. These disadvantages are strongly correlated with students' achievement (as shown in chapter 6, annex 6A, table 6A.1). Results are consistent for English, mathematics, and Chichewa.

## HOW THE REPORT EXPLORES THE DRIVERS OF LOW LEARNING

This report uses data from the MLSS baseline on a broad range of school, teacher, and student characteristics to identify the factors that drive Malawi's low performance in learning, as follows:

- "Introduction: Why Has Malawi Performed Poorly in Education?" provides a historical background to the challenges facing Malawi's primary school system and introduces the MLSS, its purpose, and procedures.
- Chapter 1, "Malawi's Low-Level Education Equilibrium," summarizes the performance of the Malawian primary school system, including levels of service, student participation, and learning outcomes. Although the system's overall performance is low, it exhibits significant variation in educational outcomes both between and within schools.
- Chapter 2, "Schools: Learning Disadvantages in Remote Schools," identifies a relationship between school remoteness and the wide inequities in school conditions, including the availability and condition of infrastructure, teaching and learning materials, financing, staffing, and supervision.
- Chapter 3, "Teachers: Learning Constraints from Large Class Sizes," focuses on teachers and teaching practices, finding that large class sizes limit the effectiveness of even skilled and highly motivated teachers.
- Chapter 4, "Students: The Importance of Home Background and Support," focuses on inequities in student populations between schools, finding that schools with high proportions of students with illiterate parents, students

speaking minority languages, over-age students, and, particularly, students with poor mindsets achieve lower learning outcomes.
- Chapter 5, "Focus on Girls' Learning," shows that student-level characteristics account for the majority of the variation in learning outcomes and that, of these characteristics, gender is associated with the biggest inequities. Quantitative and qualitative analyses find that support to female learners by school leaders and communities can reduce these gaps in learning.
- Chapter 6, "The Effects of Multiple Disadvantages on Student Achievement," presents the Disadvantage Index as a tool to understand the ways in which multiple dimensions of disadvantage interact at the school level. The chapter also models the impact of investing in low-cost classrooms and additional lower-primary teachers at the most disadvantaged schools.
- "Conclusion: The Challenge and Opportunity of Longitudinal Education Data" summarizes the findings of the MLSS baseline data, the forthcoming uses of the MLSS midline and endline data, and the ways in which the data will support promising interventions and reforms to address key constraints to learning.

## NOTES

1. In particular, the MLSS data collection is aligned with the Malawi Education Sector Improvement Project (MESIP), implemented 2016–21 with support from the Global Partnership for Education, as well as with the Malawi Education Reform Program, beginning in 2022, with support from the Global Partnership for Education and the World Bank.
2. Subsequent rounds have included the testing of more than 10,000 additional grade 4 students and retesting of more than 8,000 students from the original baseline sample.
3. Refer to the MESIP Implementation Completion and Results report for preliminary findings from evaluation of MESIP using MLSS data (World Bank 2022). Refer also to Asim and Casley Gera, forthcoming; Asim, Casley Gera, Harris, and Dercon, forthcoming; and Asim, Casley Gera, Moreno and Wang, forthcoming, for specific evaluations.
4. "Remote schools" are the 20 percent of MLSS schools farthest from the nearest trading center, whereas the 20 percent of schools closest to trading centers are defined as "schools close to a trading center." Refer to chapter 2 for more information.

## REFERENCES

Asim, S., and R. Casley Gera. Forthcoming. "Are Short-Term Gains in Learning Outcomes Possible? Evidence from the Malawi Education Sector Improvement Project." Policy Research Working Paper, World Bank, Washington, DC.

Asim, S., R. Casley Gera, D. Harris, and S. Dercon,. Forthcoming. "Does Effective School Leadership Improve Student Progression and Test Scores? Evidence from a Field Experiment in Malawi." Policy Research Working Paper, World Bank, Washington, DC.

Asim, S., R. Casley Gera, M. Moreno, and K. Wang. Forthcoming. "Can Targeted Allocation of Teachers Improve Student Learning Outcomes? Evidence from Malawi." Policy Research Working Paper, World Bank, Washington, DC.

World Bank. 2021. *The Human Capital Index 2020 Update: Human Capital in the Time of COVID-19*. Washington, DC: World Bank.

World Bank. 2022. "Implementation Completion and Results Report on an Education For All–Fast Track Initiative (EFAF) Grant (TF A2913) in the Amount of US$44.9 Million to the Republic of Malawi for the Malawi Education Sector Improvement Project (MESIP)." Report No. ICR00005716, World Bank, Washington, DC.

# Abbreviations

| | |
|---|---|
| DI | Disadvantage Index |
| DP | Development Partner |
| EGMA | Early Grade Math Assessment |
| EGRA | Early Grade Reading Assessment |
| EMIS | education management information system |
| ESIP | Education Sector Improvement Plan |
| HLM | hierarchical linear model |
| MERP | Malawi Education Reform Program |
| MESIP | Malawi Education Sector Improvement Project |
| MHM | menstrual health management |
| MLSS | Malawi Longitudinal School Survey |
| MoE | Ministry of Education |
| NESP | National Education Sector Plan |
| PCR | pupil-classroom ratio |
| PqTR | pupil-qualified teacher ratio |
| PSLCE | Primary School Leaving Certificate Examinations |
| PTR | pupil-teacher ratio |
| SACMEQ | Southern and Eastern African Consortium for Monitoring Education Quality |
| SDI | Service Delivery Indicators |
| SIG | School Improvement Grant |

# Introduction

## WHY HAS MALAWI PERFORMED POORLY IN EDUCATION?

### KEY POINTS

Malawi's primary education system represents an extreme example of "schooling without learning" (World Bank 2018). The introduction of free primary education in 1994 led to a rapid increase in access, but this increased access was accompanied by increased overcrowding and stagnation in learning outcomes. Thirty years on, the system remains highly overstretched despite investment and reform efforts, creating a status quo characterized by low levels of learning and significant inequities between schools and students.

The continuing crisis reflects the disconnect between administrative data, policy, and the on-the-ground realities individual schools face. High-quality data can help to shed light on the most severe disparities and support a more targeted approach to investment to reduce inequities and improve learning outcomes.

### LOW LEARNING LEVELS DESPITE EXPANDED SCHOOL ACCESS

The lack of improvement in test scores in Malawi reflects the education system's struggle to keep pace with the very rapid expansion of enrollment since 1994. Following the introduction of free primary education after the first multiparty elections in Malawi in 1994, the response was large and immediate, with primary enrollments surging from 1.9 million in 1993/94 to 2.8 million in 1994/95 according to Ministry of Education (MoE) administrative data. The effect on learning conditions was immediate and negative: the national pupil-teacher ratio (PTR) jumped from 88 to 1 in 1992/93 to 131 to 1 in 1994/95, and the number of students per desk rose from 32 to 56 (Kadzamira and Rose, 2001). Stopgap measures were taken to meet the sudden surge in demand, with increasing use of open-air classrooms and the appointment of so many unqualified teachers that, by 1997, more than half of all teachers were unqualified (Kadzamira and Rose, 2001).[1] In the words of former President Joyce Banda, "When we adopted Free Primary Education, we rushed. We did not know what we were going into. We compromised quality" (Wamba and Mgomezulu 2014).

The continuing poor conditions in schools led to low levels of learning. Malawian students performed less well than students in other countries in the region, in both reading and mathematics, in learning assessments by the Southern and Eastern African Consortium for Monitoring Education Quality in both 2002 and 2007 (Ravishankar et al. 2016). As a result, parents demanded that students repeat grades to ensure they reached a minimum level of grade-level proficiency, with the result that repetition rates increased rapidly, to 23 percent by 2014 (Kadzamira and Chibwana 2000; World Bank 2016). These high rates of repetition further inflated enrollments: by 2016, 4.9 million children—more than one-fifth of Malawi's entire population—were enrolled in primary school. This continuing rapid expansion put further pressure on underresourced schools. In 2015, the average pupil-classroom ratio (PCR) was higher (126 to 1) than in 1997 (119 to 1) despite large capital investments in the primary education sector since that year, and class sizes of more than 150 pupils were commonplace in lower grades (Kadzamira and Rose 2001; World Bank 2016).

By 2016, despite intensive efforts by the government and substantial investment by development partners, Malawi's education system had become stuck in a low-level equilibrium. The Malawi Longitudinal School Survey (MLSS) baseline data show that, in 2016, schools were experiencing daily student absence rates of 29 percent, grade repetition rates of 20 percent, and dropout rates of 6 percent. By grade 4, students struggled with even basic items in key subjects, suggesting a severe crisis of learning (as discussed in chapter 1).

## INSUFFICIENT, INADEQUATELY TARGETED FINANCING AND WEAK DATA SYSTEMS

Why have subsequent waves of reform and investment failed to raise learning outcomes? Analysis of the most recently completed sector plan and its implementation demonstrates some of the key challenges. Following the initial period of rapid expansion, attention began to shift in the late 2000s to the issues of quality and learning outcomes. The National Education Sector Plan (NESP) for 2008–17 established as the strategic priority of the education sector in Malawi *the improvement of quality, equity, relevance, access, and efficiency of basic education*. The NESP was supported by extensive development partner investment and significant new initiatives to target improvement in school conditions, such as School Improvement Grants, the first discretionary financing available to schools to invest in teaching and learning materials and improvements in learning environments. However, the NESP, associated five-year Education Sector Improvement Plans, and the related development partner projects exhibited common weaknesses of large-scale investment programs in low-income countries—providing ambitious policy recommendations, without adequate financing, and with insufficient targeting of resources to maximize the impact of the limited financing available.

### High costs and inadequate financing

The ambitious goals of Malawi's NESP were a product of what Andrews, Pritchett, and Woolcock (2012) describe as "isomorphic mimicry," or "the tendency to introduce reforms that enhance an entity's external legitimacy and support, even when they do not demonstrably improve performance." The NESP goals met international expectations but were prohibitively expensive and resource-intensive for Malawi's capacity-constrained context.[2] For example, the government's standard model of school classrooms, which imitates the class infrastructure of a school in an Organisation for Economic Co-operation and Development country, cost an average US$23,500 per classroom to construct (World Bank 2019). The NESP 2008–17 called for construction of 27,000 new classrooms at public schools between 2006 and 2017; at the prevailing cost, this construction would have a cost of US$635 million—twice the total annual education budget. This top-level target was never incorporated into the associated Education Sector Improvement Plans, both of which set a less ambitious goal of 1,500 classrooms per year, although even this reduced goal was not met. Similarly, although the introduction of School Improvement Grants was an important step in providing development financing for schools, the level of per-student financing was extremely low: less than US$1.20 per student per year,[3] which is less than half the amount spent in Tanzania (Mbiti et al. 2019) or Zambia (World Bank 2022). The combination of limited financing and high-cost models meant that schools were unable to address infrastructure shortages through School Improvement Grants at a pace of more than one classroom every several years.

### Inadequate targeting of limited resources

Unrealistic national-level goals have created an environment in which the limited resources available are insufficiently targeted to schools in the greatest need. For example, the national PCR goal is 60 to 1, yet 82 percent of schools fall short of this target. As a consequence, the target was ineffective at prioritizing the most overcrowded schools for investment, and relatively privileged schools benefited; if all the new classrooms constructed during the period 2013–17 had been targeted to the neediest one-fifth of schools, the PCR for these schools would have fallen from 196 to 1 in 2013 to about 134 to 1 in 2017. Instead, only half the new classrooms constructed at existing schools were provided to the least-equipped schools. The result was that the disparity in PCRs remained large, with the neediest schools having an average 167 students per classroom and the best-equipped 55 students per classroom, according to 2017 MoE education management information system (EMIS) data.

The gap between the available infrastructure and the need is larger than ever: according to the MLSS baseline, to raise all rural schools to a PCR of 60 to 1 would require construction of more than 37,000 classrooms at a cost of US$875 million.[4] The official PTR goal is also 60 to 1; about three-quarters of schools fall short of the target[5] and require an average of four additional teachers to meet the goal. Raising all rural schools to meet the target, without removing teachers from schools that are currently well-staffed, would require the hiring of an additional 13,500 teachers at a cost of US$15.4 million per year.[6]

### Inadequate quality and quantity of data

Well-intentioned reforms to improve the quality of learning in Malawi have been limited by ineffective implementation due to a lack of reliable data. For example, Malawi introduced a hardship support scheme in 2010 to address inequities in school staffing by rewarding teachers who accept postings in remote areas with limited amenities, which have PTRs more than double that of schools close to well-equipped trading centers. The policy was originally intended to reward about 15,000 teachers—less than one-third of the total at the time—with a sum equivalent to about one-third of an average teacher's salary. However, when the scheme was implemented, the absence of reliable indicators of hardship made it difficult to target allowances effectively and the initial rollout included more than half of Malawi's teachers. Successive rounds of legal and industrial action (by teachers who had been ruled ineligible) further expanded the pool of entitled teachers until, by 2015, 80 percent of teachers were eligible for the allowance and its value had shrunk to about one-seventh the average teacher salary, negating any incentive effect. Despite the idea's successful implementation in other countries, insufficient data led to an expensive failure, which deepened misallocations of resources rather than reducing them (Evans and Acosta 2021). However, new reforms have introduced a new definition of school hardship grounded in accurate and up-to-date data on the placement of teachers (Asim et al. 2019), and a new, more fully targeted support scheme based on this categorization is being rolled out in 2024 (refer to box I.1).

The overemphasis on headline policies over the details of targeting and enforcement is an example of a wider tendency in low- and middle-income

---

**BOX I.1**

### Malawi Education Reform Program

Malawi Longitudinal School Survey data informed priorities for the Malawi Education Reform Program (MERP). The successor program to the Malawi Education Sector Improvement Project, MERP is being implemented from 2022 to 2025 with finance from the Global Partnership for Education and the World Bank. The design has been heavily informed by the survey findings and focuses on providing targeted support to the neediest schools and students in several ways:

- *Reform of School Improvement Grants.* MERP expands School Improvement Grants and supports a new formula targeting more financing to remote schools and those with a small share of students with pre-primary education (as discussed in chapter 4). Results-based finance rewards the government for timely release of the grants to schools, reducing delays that often impede efficient investment in infrastructure and materials (as discussed in chapter 2).
- *Community construction of low-cost classrooms and hiring of teachers.* Schools with severe shortages of classrooms or teachers in lower-primary grades receive grant financing to construct low-cost classrooms and hire auxiliary teachers. Levels of financing are tied to the severity of shortages, with the most disadvantaged schools—those with a pupil-classroom ratio above 90 to 1—eligible to construct six classrooms and hire four additional auxiliary teachers. It is anticipated that this support will reduce the share of schools with severe overcrowding in lower primary by more than half.
- *Hardship support scheme.* MERP supports the introduction of a revised hardship support scheme for teachers working in remote schools, employing a new objective data-driven definition of remoteness. Teachers working in the approximately one-third of schools that are most remote—those far from a trading center and lacking school facilities—will receive an additional payment equivalent to more than one-fifth their usual salary. Unlike the former unsuccessful allowance scheme, the revised scheme will employ a strict fact-based categorization of remoteness (Asim et al. 2019) and provide financing via schools, ensuring that only teachers actively employed at a school receive the allowance.
- *Support for girls' learning.* To support equitable learning for girls, MERP scales up an existing *learner mentors* program, through which secondary school graduates mentor female learners. In addition, district-level action plans support improved placement of female teachers in remote schools, and results-based financing supports gender-disaggregated reporting on student test scores to schools to raise awareness of gender inequities in learning.
- *School Leadership Program.* This program, introduced under the Malawi Education Sector Improvement Project (refer to box I.2) is also being scaled up under MERP and is expected to reach all school leaders by 2025.

countries to focus on policy choice and underemphasize implementation, including a failure to collect the data necessary to learn what is working and why (Andrews, Pritchett, and Woolcock 2012; Duflo 2017).

To develop reliable sources of data, donors and governments worldwide have invested heavily in recent years in EMISs; however, most systems face serious challenges of data quality and of data being held in EMIS departments and not widely used (World Bank 2018). In Malawi, the World Bank–supported Project to Improve Education Quality (2010–15) invested heavily in improving the quality of EMIS data through training and the introduction of district-level EMIS officers. Despite improvements, however, EMIS data remained insufficiently accurate to serve as a reliable source for targeting or even for providing monitoring and evaluation data for the project itself (World Bank 2016). Without a high-quality source of school-level data, policy makers had to rely on poor-quality data drawing from inconsistent and problematic samples that ultimately depicted a different reality than what was on the ground. As a result, policy makers struggled to implement effective reforms.

## PERSISTENCE OF SIGNIFICANT INEQUITIES IN LEARNING OUTCOMES BETWEEN SCHOOLS

The result of these weaknesses in planning and implementation is that Malawi's education system is not only marred by poor overall outcomes but also marked by huge disparities between schools. Malawi's primary schools have an overall average PTR of 67 to 1, according to 2019 MoE EMIS data; however, on average, the most understaffed school in a zone has a PTR five times higher than the best-staffed (Asim et al. 2019). In an average zone, PCRs range from 45 pupils to a classroom to 158, reflecting a huge variance in classroom overcrowding within the same neighborhood.

These disparities can be illustrated by the stories of two children in two MLSS case study schools. John Nyungwe,[7] 12 years old, is a typical grade 4 student in Kamulindeni public primary school in the Vazala zone of Mzimba district, in southern Malawi. Eliya Phiri, also 12, is a grade 4 student at Chamkoko, another public primary school in the Vazala zone. Although they are both in the fourth grade, these students have very different levels of learning. In English, mathematics, and Chichewa learning assessments, John scored an average of 38 percent across subjects, whereas Eliya scored just 21 percent. These students' divergent outcomes are indicative of their schools, which have widely divergent conditions and outcomes even though both are in the same subdistrict area (table I.1). John and Eliya's stories are indicative of the crisis of inequity in Malawi's public school system.

## INSIGHTS FOR NEW POLICY DIRECTIONS FROM THE MALAWI LONGITUDINAL SCHOOL SURVEY

To provide Malawi with accurate and precise data on a wide range of school-level conditions, practices, and outcomes, the MoE developed the MLSS in partnership with the World Bank and with financing from the Royal Norwegian Embassy and the United Kingdom Foreign, Commonwealth and Development Office. The MLSS is a first attempt to anchor education policy choices and sector dialogue firmly in

TABLE I.1 **Comparison of conditions and learning outcomes in two schools within the same zone**

| CHARACTERISTIC | KAMULINDENI SCHOOL | CHAMKOKO SCHOOL |
|---|---|---|
| Overall knowledge score[a] | 497 | 395 |
| Same zone | Vazala zone, Mzimba South district | |
| Number of disadvantages[b] | 1 | 4 |
| Distance to trading center (kilometers) | 7.3 | 13.3 |
| Pupil-teacher ratio | 50 to 1 | 84 to 1 |
| Ratio of female pupils to female teachers | 35 to 1 | 109 to 1 |
| Grade 4 average class size | 34 students | 44 students |
| Share of junior teachers[c] (%) | 43 | 60 |
| Pupil-classroom ratio | 59 to 1 | 70 to 1 |
| Share of classrooms in need of repair[d] (%) | 0 | 86 |
| Pupil-textbook ratio | 1.9 to 1 | 4.0 to 1 |
| Share of students with pencil and notebook (%) | 100 | 79 |
| Share of students with uniform (%) | 84 | 11 |
| Share of students in psychological poverty[e] (%) | 40 | 72 |
| Share of minority-language students (%) | 64 | 80 |
| Share of students with own bed (%) | 48 | 24 |

*Source:* Malawi Longitudinal School Survey baseline (2016) data, World Bank.
a. For information on construction of the knowledge score, refer to box I.3.
b. The Disadvantage Index includes any of the following: School is more than 10 kilometers from the nearest trading center; school meets three or four shortage conditions for student learning materials; school has no females among the head teacher, deputy head teacher, section heads, School Management Committee chair and vice chair, or parent-teacher association chair and vice chair; school has both a pupil-teacher ratio and pupil-classroom ratio above 90 to 1; and fewer than 30 percent of school's students have one or more year of pre-primary education.
c. Junior teachers include PT4 (most junior qualified teaching level), student teachers, and teaching assistants (as discussed in chapter 3).
d. "In need of repair" refers to a classroom whose walls, floor, or roof is not in fine condition.
e. For a detailed definition of psychological poverty, refer to chapter 4, figure 4.2.

school-level data. It provides a deep dive into a nationally representative sample of schools, complementing and supporting the EMIS in several ways:

- *Accuracy.* MLSS data are collected by independent, Malawi-based research firms through unannounced visits to schools, providing the most objective and accurate picture of conditions and practices in schools. MLSS data have supported the validation and further improvement of EMIS data.
- *Scope.* The MLSS includes information on a vast range of indicators not included in the annual school census (the primary source of EMIS data), including student and teacher attendance, teaching practices, management and supervision practices, and student and teacher attitudes and experiences. Most important, the MLSS provides robust measurement of grade 4 learning outcomes, providing accurate benchmarking of system-level learning in a large national sample of schools for the first time.[8]
- *Longitudinal data.* In addition to the baseline data presented in this report, the MLSS provides longitudinal data on school conditions and practices and student learning trajectories over time, enabling evaluation of education interventions (refer to box I.2).

## BOX I.2

### The MLSS as longitudinal survey

In addition to providing the most detailed picture to date of conditions, practices, and outcomes in a nationally representative sample of Malawi's public primary schools, the Malawi Longitudinal School Survey (MLSS) provides longitudinal data on the same schools and students over multiple rounds. The MLSS's longitudinal design is a key feature that distinguishes it from the World Bank's Service Delivery Indicators and education management information system data.

A longitudinal study gathers data about respondents over a period of time, enabling it to collect more complete, chronologically ordered, and detailed information on respondents than that collected by a one-off survey or cross-sectional study (Park and Rainsberry 2020). In education, longitudinal data from students and schools enable researchers and policy makers to track levels of learning, understand the trajectories of children's learning over time, and identify how education systems are performing over time (Muralidharan 2013). Such detailed longitudinal data from students and schools are critical in low-resource contexts because they are necessary for identifying possible reasons for low levels of learning. Hypotheses based on those insights can then be tested through randomized controlled trials, creating a cycle of intervention testing and evaluation.

**The longitudinal sample**

The MLSS's full longitudinal sample includes 924 schools, of which 750 underwent baseline data collection between May 2016 and July 2018.[a] Midline data collection was conducted in 403 schools between November 2018 and December 2019, with the sample aligned to support impact evaluations of Malawi Education Sector Improvement Project (MESIP) interventions (discussed later in this box). Endline data collection was completed in 659 schools during 2021/22, providing a complete nationally representative endline sample. In each school, students sampled at baseline are reinterviewed and undergo repeat learning assessments in each round, providing detailed information on the trajectories of learning over time.

**Impact evaluations**

The MLSS baseline, midline, and endline surveys were linked to the project cycle of MESIP, a large-scale government investment project implemented from December 2016 to July 2021 with financial support from the Global Partnership for Education, and an extension project, MESIP-Extended, supported by the Royal Norwegian Embassy. The MLSS sample is overlaid onto the randomized sample for these pilots enabling rigorous experimental evaluation. MESIP evaluations included the following:

- *Overall evaluation.* The MESIP interventions were interconnected, with the majority focused in eight disadvantaged districts of Malawi. The evaluation demonstrates that the project closed historic gaps in learning between these and other districts.
- *School Leadership Program.* About 1,200 head teachers, along with their deputies and Primary Education Advisers (subdistrict education officials), participated in a multiyear program to raise skills in resource management, record-keeping, teacher management, and the creation of inclusive school cultures. Initial results show strong impacts on learning for older students driven by improvements in the provision of remedial classes.
- *Community information and engagement using information and communication technology.* The 1,200 schools received monthly visits from zonal education management information system officers to collect data on key performance indicators, disseminated to communities via short message service texts and printed report cards; 1,200 other schools were enrolled into a text-based system for dialogue around education.

Selected findings from these evaluations will be published in 2024.

*continued*

**Box I.2**, *continued*

**Malawi Education Reform Program**
In addition, the MLSS midline has already been used to inform the design of the Malawi Education Reform Program, the successor program to MESIP (as discussed in box I.1).

**COVID-19 learning loss**
Data from all three MLSS rounds have also been used to prepare preliminary analysis of learning loss resulting from COVID-19. The analysis was presented to the government in June 2022 and is scheduled for publication during 2024.

a. This report presents findings from the first phase of baseline, conducted in 2016, which included 559 schools.

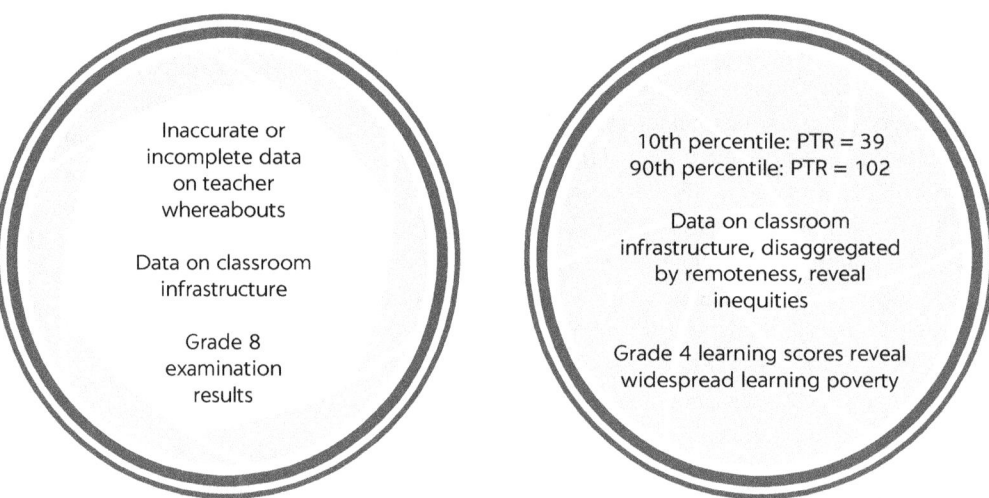

FIGURE I.1
**The administrative data lens versus the MLSS data lens**

a. Administrative data: A broad picture
- Inaccurate or incomplete data on teacher whereabouts
- Data on classroom infrastructure
- Grade 8 examination results

b. MLSS data: A detailed picture
- 10th percentile: PTR = 39
- 90th percentile: PTR = 102
- Data on classroom infrastructure, disaggregated by remoteness, reveal inequities
- Grade 4 learning scores reveal widespread learning poverty

*Source:* Original figure for this publication.
*Note:* "Teacher whereabouts" refers to both *teacher placement* (administrative data are of low quality and incomplete) and *teacher absence* (completely missing from administrative data). "10th percentile" refers to the highest-performing schools in terms of PTR, that is, the smallest class size, and "90th percentile" to the lowest-performing schools (largest class size). "Learning poverty" is the inability to read and understand a simple text by age 10. MLSS = Malawi Longitudinal School Survey; PTR = pupil-teacher ratio.

The MLSS provides a detailed picture of a representative sample of schools, which in turn provides more accurate measures of indicators that have historically been prone to inaccurate recording in the EMIS (such as the placement of teachers)[9] and captures a wider range of indicators, such as classroom conditions as well as test scores for grade 4 students. To use the metaphor of a camera, administrative data is a lens that creates a low-resolution picture of the education system to inform macro investments in the sector, whereas the MLSS is a high-resolution lens that allows policy makers to create a sharp, more robust picture of school-level conditions and student learning trajectories (figure I.1). Whereas a lack of reliable school-level data has created a disconnect between official policy and the on-the-ground reality of schools, the MLSS provides

MAP I.1
**Malawian primary schools included in the MLSS baseline sample, 2016**

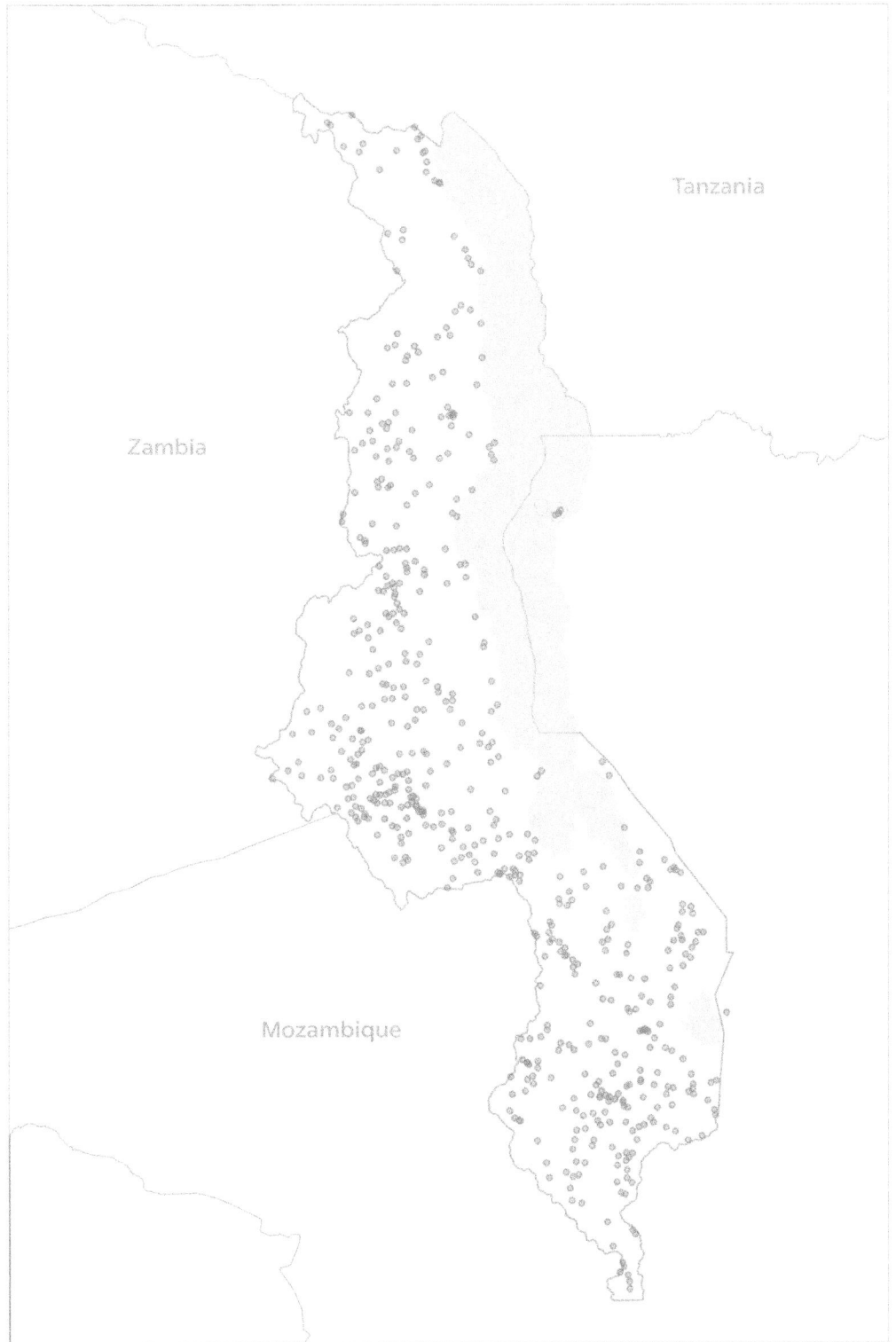

Source: World Bank.
Note: Red dots indicate schools included in the survey. MLSS = Malawi Longitudinal School Survey.

> **BOX I.3**
>
> ### The MLSS learning assessments and knowledge scores
>
> The Malawi Longitudinal School Survey (MLSS) includes norm-referenced learning assessments in English, mathematics, and Chichewa for sampled students in grade 4. The MLSS assessments contain items aligned with the curricula for each of grades 1 to 6. To reflect this variation in difficulty of items, the MLSS assigns *knowledge scores* to each student for each subject. To create the knowledge score, scores are adapted to a mean-centered scale centered at 500 using item response theory, which assigns value to each item based on the likelihood of its being answered correctly. Knowledge scores across the three subjects are then averaged to produce an overall knowledge score for each student, which can then be averaged at the school level or for other groupings of students. Throughout this report, unless otherwise specified, "knowledge score" denotes overall knowledge score. For more detail, refer to the online technical appendix (https://openknowledge.worldbank.org/handle/10986/40948).

insights grounded in granular data on students, teachers, and communities that enable policy makers to develop new perspectives for education policy reforms.

The MLSS was designed to collect data in three rounds from a representative sample of Malawian primary schools. This baseline report provides findings from the initial baseline round of MLSS conducted in 2016. Subsequent evaluation reports will provide updated information capturing the impact of key interventions and the changes in student learning trajectories over time.

The initial baseline survey was conducted in 559 primary schools in all districts of Malawi (509 in rural areas)[10] (map I.1) and collected a wide range of information on conditions, practices, and learning outcomes in schools (refer to box I.3). Data collection, conducted through unannounced visits,[11] included interviews with more than 10,000 head teachers, teachers, and community members, as well as learning assessments and interviews with more than 13,000 students (refer to appendix A of this volume).

The baseline MLSS data have been used extensively to inform and support the government since 2016. A summary report of baseline findings was prepared and shared with MoE management in October 2019 (Asim, Gera, and Wang 2019), along with a presentation of key findings in December 2019. The findings informed the preparation of the new National Education Sector Investment Plan 2020–30, in particular supporting inclusion of equity targets for PCR and PTR for the first time in a Malawi national education sector plan.

Although the baseline was conducted in 2016, for the purposes of clarity, the remainder of this report will use the present tense when describing findings. Initial analysis of midline and endline data suggests some improvements in some key areas since 2016, including in learning inequities, as a result of investments including the Malawi Education Sector Improvement Project (refer to box I.2) and the National Reading Programme (refer to the Conclusion chapter of this book). However, the dynamics of which school and student characteristics matter for learning, which are the focus of this report, remain largely unchanged. Forthcoming data from the midline and endline rounds of MLSS will further support policy making through impact evaluation of recent interventions and estimation of learning loss resulting from the COVID-19 pandemic.

## NOTES

1. By comparison, only 16 percent in 1993/4 were unqualified (Kadzamira and Rose 2001).
2. Whereas discussion of state capacity in political science has often focused on the capacity of states to raise taxes, in a low-income context in which donor financing provides a significant share of government revenue, it is more relevant to consider the capacity of the state to *spend* revenue equitably, effectively, and in line with political and policy goals (Besley and Persson 2009; Khemani 2019; Tilly 1990).
3. The MLSS baseline-sampled schools received MK 878 (US$1.19) per student in 2015/16.
4. We calculate the units required to achieve the PCR target at MLSS schools and extrapolate to remaining rural schools on a per-district basis, using the prevailing cost as previously cited.
5. Only 27 percent of schools have a ratio of pupils to qualified teachers below 60 to 1. If nonqualified teachers are included, 42 percent of schools have a PTR below 60 to 1.
6. We use average 2016 teacher salary from MLSS teacher interviews and extrapolate to the national level.
7. Names have been changed; ages are at time of baseline survey.
8. Comparable data on student learning have historically been available only through the Primary School Leaving Certificate Examination conducted in grade 8. The MLSS sample is substantially larger than those used by the Southern and Eastern African Consortium for Monitoring Education Quality and other regional studies.
9. EMIS data on the working location of teachers have been historically of poor quality, although they have improved significantly in recent years (Asim et al. 2019).
10. In general, descriptive statistics presented in the text are for all sampled schools; however, the regression analyses and select figures are estimated specifically for rural schools because of differences in conditions between urban and rural schools, the latter of which account for about 80–90 percent of enrollment.
11. Data collection was conducted through unannounced visits to schools to obtain a true picture of everyday conditions and practices. Additional, announced visits were conducted, as well as telephone calls, to complete data collection that was not possible to complete during the unannounced visit.

## REFERENCES

Andrews, M., L. Pritchett, and M. Woolcock. 2012. "Escaping Capability Traps through Problem Driven Iterative Adaptation (PDIA)." Faculty Research Working Paper 12-036, John F. Kennedy School of Government, Cambridge, MA.

Asim, S., J. Chimombo, D. Chugunov, and R. Gera. 2019. "Moving Teachers to Malawi's Remote Communities: A Data-Driven Approach to Teacher Deployment." *International Journal of Educational Development* 65: 26–43.

Asim, S., R. Gera, and X. Wang. 2019. "Creating Equal Opportunities for Malawi's Children: Insights from a Longitudinal School Survey." Unpublished manuscript, World Bank, Washington, DC.

Besley, T., and T. Persson. 2009. "The Origins Of State Capacity: Property Rights, Taxation and Politics." *American Economic Review* 99 (4): 1218–44.

Duflo, E. 2017. "The Economist as Plumber." Working Paper 23213, National Bureau of Economic Research, Cambridge, MA.

Evans, D., and A. Acosta. 2021. "How to Recruit Teachers for Hard-to-Staff Schools: A Systematic Review of Evidence from Low- and Middle-Income Countries." Working Paper 595, Center for Global Development, Washington, DC.

Kadzamira, E. C., and M. P. Chibwana. 2000. "Gender and Primary Schooling in Malawi." Research Report 40, Institute of Development Studies, Brighton, UK.

Kadzamira, E., and P. Rose. 2001. "Educational Policy Choice and Policy Practice in Malawi: Dilemmas and Disjunctures." Working Paper 124, Institute of Development Studies, Brighton, UK.

Khemani, S. 2019. "What Is State Capacity?" Policy Research Working Paper 8734, World Bank, Washington, DC.

Mbiti, I., K. Muralidharan, M. Romero, Y. Schipper, C. Manda, and R. Rajani. 2019. "Inputs, Incentives, and Complementarities in Education: Experimental Evidence from Tanzania." *Quarterly Journal of Economics* 134 (3): 1627–73.

Muralidharan, K. 2013. "Inequalities 2013: Karthik Muralidharan on Measuring Learning Trajectories with Longitudinal Data." YouTube video. https://www.youtube.com/watch?v=bkLMZKh4WBE.

Park, A., and M. Rainsberry. 2020. "Strengths of Longitudinal Data." In "Introduction to Longitudinal Studies," Online module, Learning Hub, University College London (UCL) Institute of Education, London. https://learning.closer.ac.uk/learning-modules/introduction/what-can-longitudinal-studies-show-us/strengths-of-longitudinal-studies/.

Ravishankar, V., S. E. T. El-Kogali, D. Sankar, N. Tanaka, and N. Rakoto-Tiana. 2016. *Primary Education in Malawi: Expenditures, Service Delivery and Outcomes.* Washington, DC: World Bank.

Tilly, C. 1990. *Coercion, Capital, and European States, AD 990-1990 (Studies in Social Discontinuity).* Cambridge: Blackwell.

Wamba, N., and V. Mgomezulu. 2014. "The Crisis in Public Education in Malawi." *International Journal of Advanced Research* 2 (4): 323–31.

World Bank. 2016. "International Development Association Project Appraisal Document on a Proposed Grant in the Amount of US$44.9 Million to the Republic of Malawi for a Malawi Education Sector Improvement Project (MESIP)." Report No. PAD1515, World Bank, Washington, DC.

World Bank. 2018. *World Development Report 2018: Learning to Realize Education's Promise.* Washington, DC: World Bank.

World Bank. 2019. "International Development Association Project Appraisal Document on a Proposed Grant in the Amount of SDR 64/8 Million (US$90 Million Equivalent) to the Republic of Malawi for the Equity with Quality and Learning at Secondary Project (EQUALS)." Report No. PAD2918, World Bank, Washington, DC.

World Bank. 2022. "Financing Basic Education: The Financial Implications of Zambia's 'Education for All' Policy." Zambia Education Knowledge Brief 2-2022, World Bank, Washington, DC.

# 1 Malawi's Low-Level Education Equilibrium

## KEY POINTS

Baseline data from the Malawi Longitudinal School Survey (MLSS) show that Malawi's education system has settled into a status quo with low levels of learning, and with the system's performance aligning with capacity rather than official policy. Although rapidly increasing access has led to extremely large official enrollments, high absenteeism means that the levels of schooling are lower than official statistics suggest. Rates of repetition and dropout are extremely high, and students who do advance to upper grades often demonstrate learning outcomes well below those expected. The disconnect between official policy and the reality presented by the MLSS demonstrates the need for high-quality, independent data that can be used to set new policy directions.

## LOW SERVICE STANDARDS AND HIGH STUDENT ABSENTEEISM IN PRIMARY SCHOOLS

Malawi's primary schools are characterized by low standards of service and high rates of student absence. MLSS baseline data show that Malawi's primary schools fall consistently short of official standards of service. Official policies set standards for schooling that the system has consistently struggled to meet in most schools. As described in the introduction to this report, 75–85 percent of schools fall short of the official targets for pupil-classroom ratio (PCR) and pupil-teacher ratio. Only 1 in 10 schools achieves a PCR of 60 to 1 in grade 1, where classes tend to be largest.[1]

Malawi's schools also face significant constraints in providing quality learning environments. Twenty-nine percent of schools conduct open-air classes, an average of two per school, suggesting significant shortages of physical buildings. Including open-air classes, the typical class size is 95, and severe overcrowding is quite common. Most schools (81 percent) lack electricity, and the typical school has limited handwashing and hygiene facilities, with one toilet for every 77 pupils. The physical infrastructure that is available is often in need of repair: on average, more than a third of school classrooms have walls that are cracked, damaged, or broken; a fifth have a roof that is leaking or cracked; and more than half have a floor that is uneven or has cracks or holes.[2] Only 24 percent of classrooms at an average school have a corner for learning materials, and only 41 percent of students have a chair or desk.

Parents have responded to this failure of supply with reduced demand. Levels of demand for schooling in low- and middle-income countries are lower in contexts of poor quality, particularly with regard to attendance and dropout (Bergmann 1996). The MLSS baseline data show this to be the case for Malawi. In a typical Malawian primary school, 29 percent of enrolled students were absent on the day of baseline data collection.[3] Absence rates are highest in lower grades: despite the apparent overenrollment in grade 1—with a grade gross enrollment ratio of about 150 percent—35 percent of grade 1 students are absent on a typical day.[4] As in other countries (Tran and Gershenson 2021), absence rates are highest in the largest classes: classes with 90 students enrolled have 2.6 percentage points greater absenteeism than classes with 60 students on average; classes with 120 students have 4 percentage points greater absenteeism.

The MLSS findings suggest that, following the failure of the system to fulfill the goal of universal education of adequate quality, Malawian communities have responded to shortages and limitations of school supply by reducing demand to a level that schools can more adequately sustain. The result of this demand-side response to the failure of supply is that, even in schools where official enrollments most severely exceed capacity, the daily attendance of students is more aligned with the capabilities of the school. PCRs, pupil-teacher ratios, and pupil-latrine ratios at the typical school are substantially lower when measured by pupil headcount than by enrollment, albeit still above official standards (refer to figure 1.1).

FIGURE 1.1

**Ratios of pupils to classrooms, teachers, and latrines in primary schools, 2016**

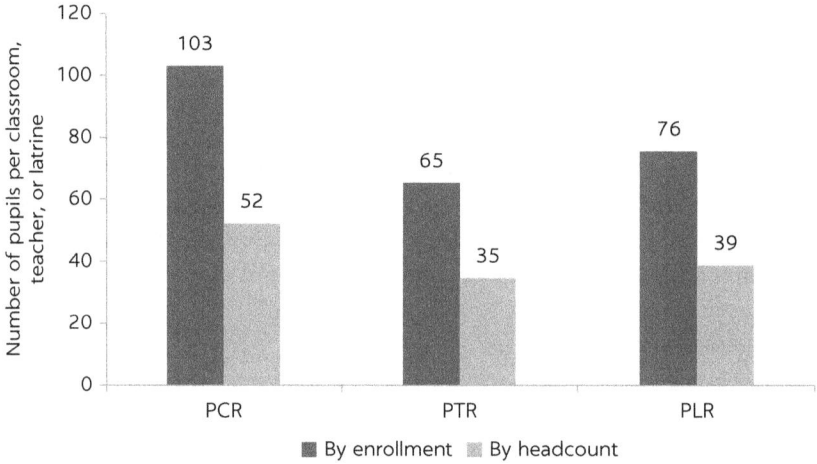

Source: Malawi Longitudinal School Survey baseline (2016) data, World Bank.
Note: "Enrollment" refers to total pupils enrolled, and "headcount" to total pupil attendance reflecting absenteeism. PCR = pupil-classroom ratio; PLR = pupil-latrine ratio; PTR = pupil-teacher ratio.

## PERSISTENCE OF HIGH REPETITION AND DROPOUT RATES

High repetition exacerbates overcrowding in lower grades. Repetition is a central feature of Malawi's education system, with all grades in most schools carrying out testing to control promotion to the next grade. A typical MLSS school has a repetition rate of 20 percent, a higher rate than other low-income African countries including Cameroon, Côte D'Ivoire, and Namibia.[5] Repetition is highest in lower grades: 22 percent of students repeat in a typical grade 1 class, which is equivalent to 36 students repeating each year in a typical grade 1 class of 163 students. These high rates of repetition exacerbate overcrowding, trapping students in crowded classes with minimal teacher attention—a vicious cycle that fails students and wastes a large amount of teaching resources.

With limited attention from teachers and high rates of absence, many students simply drop out. The grade 1 dropout rate in MLSS-sampled schools was 6 percent in 2016. This rate suggests that, of approximately 1.1 million new students enrolled in Malawi's primary schools each year, 66,000 will not make it further than the very first grade. Dropout rates remain above 5 percent throughout lower primary. These high dropout rates, combined with high repetition, mean that only 70–80 percent of students typically progress to the next grade at the end of a given year (refer to figure 1.2). The result is that, of those students who enroll in grade 1, fewer than two-thirds will make it to grade 4, and fewer than one-third will reach grade 8.

FIGURE 1.2
**Effects of dropout and repetition rates on students' progression to higher grades**

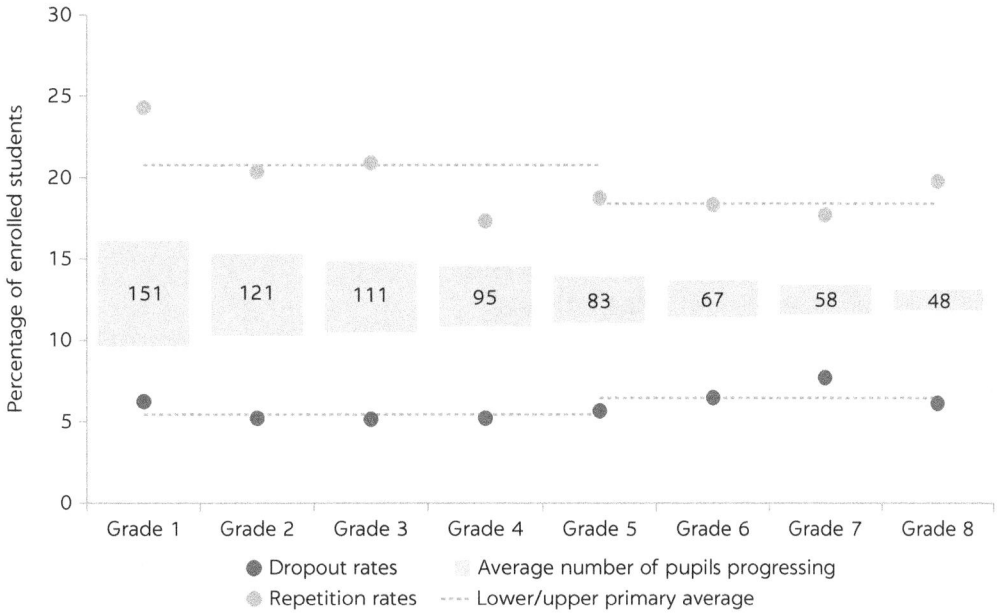

● Dropout rates   ▫ Average number of pupils progressing
◦ Repetition rates   ---- Lower/upper primary average

*Source:* World Bank calculations from Malawi Longitudinal School Survey internal baseline (2016) data.
*Note:* "Average number of pupils progressing" is the number of students enrolled in that grade for the next year who are not repeaters. "Lower/upper primary average" refers to the mean repetition or dropout rate in grades 1–4 (for lower primary) and grades 5–8 (for upper primary).

## LOW LEARNING ACHIEVEMENT

Students who do advance to grade 4 appear to have learned little. The MLSS learning assessments contain items aligned with the curricula for each of grades 1 to 6 (refer to box I.3 in the introduction to this book), enabling even students who are lagging behind to complete some tasks. The results of the assessments suggest that many students are struggling to complete even basic tasks in mathematics and English (refer to figure 1.3).

Students struggle with items from even the grade 1–2 curricula. The MLSS learning assessments' alignment with grade curricula enables us to measure the performance of students on items aligned to a particular grade (refer to figure 1.4). Most students achieved less than 50 percent in English, even on items aligned with the grade 1–2 curricula. Only about one-third of students achieved more than 50 percent on items aligned with the grade 3–4 curricula in Chichewa, 40 percent in mathematics, and just 5 percent in English. This finding suggests that, despite the high repetition rates, many students are reaching grade 4 without the expected competencies and, in some cases, without even basic skills.

A minority of grade 4 students appears to have learned almost nothing: about 15 percent of students achieved a score of zero on grade 1 items in each subject.[6]

These low learning outcomes suggest widespread learning poverty. The World Bank has set a new target of reducing learning poverty by half by 2030 (World Bank 2019). *Learning poverty* means being unable to read and understand a simple text by age 10. Although the MLSS learning assessments were developed before the introduction of the learning poverty concept, our English and Chichewa assessments, administered to students with a median age of 11,

### FIGURE 1.3

**Share of students who can perform basic mathematics and English tasks by end of grade 4, 2016**

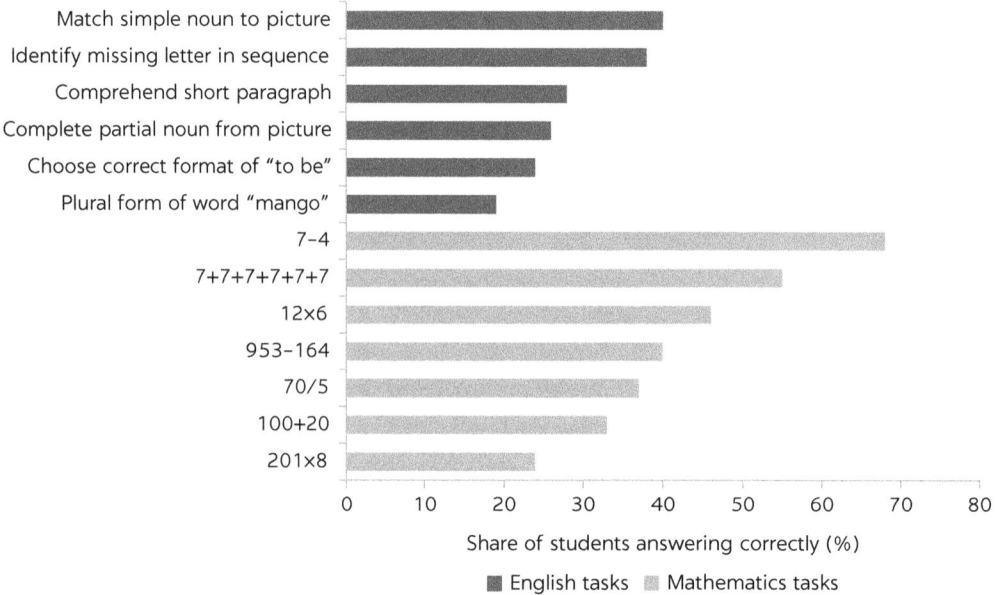

*Source:* Malawi Longitudinal School Survey baseline (2016) data, World Bank.

#### FIGURE 1.4
**Shares of grade 4 students who correctly complete tasks, by subject and grade-level curriculum, 2016**

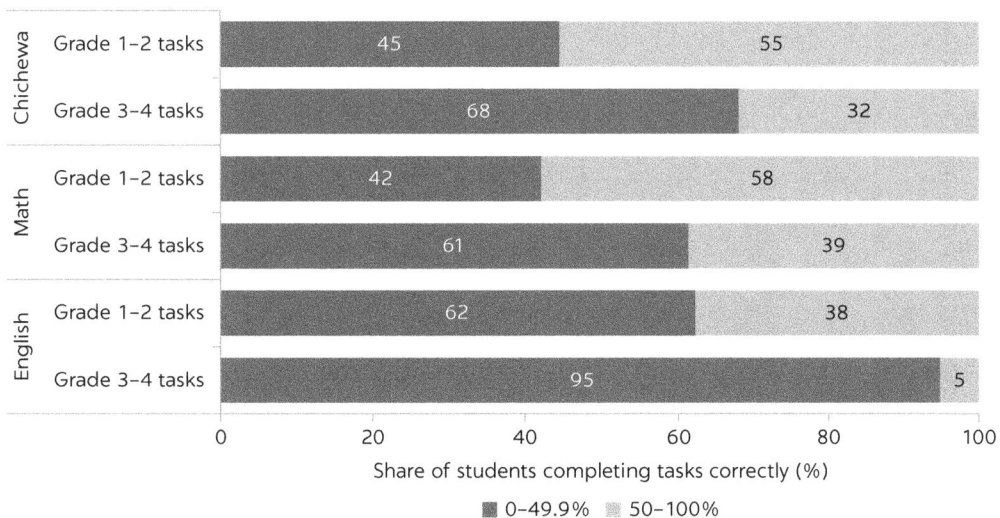

*Source:* World Bank calculations from Malawi Longitudinal School Survey baseline (2016) data.

include questions based on comprehension of a short passage. On average, 22 percent of students answered the Chichewa comprehension question correctly, suggesting a high incidence of learning poverty.

## PERSISTENCE OF INEQUITABLE OUTCOMES BETWEEN AND WITHIN SCHOOLS

Student participation and learning outcomes both vary widely between schools. Gaps in student participation between the highest-performing 10 percent of schools and lowest-performing 10 percent stretch as wide as 42 percentage points or more for absenteeism (refer to figure 1.5, panel a). A similar trend emerges in learning outcomes (refer to figure 1.5, panel b). The difference in average learning outcomes between the lowest-performing 10 percent of schools and the highest-performing is equivalent to about three years' difference in learning.[7] These large disparities persist across subjects.[8] For summary statistics, refer to annex 1A, table 1A.1.

Within schools, student learning outcomes vary enormously, with the lowest-performing students in a typical class lagging more than two years behind the highest-performing in learning. Despite the wide range of variation in school conditions, 73 percent of the variation observed in learning outcomes was found between individual grade 4 students within a school (refer to chapter 5), a greater level of within-school variation than in several other African countries.[9] Figure 1.6 shows the distribution in knowledge scores for each subject among sampled students from the typical school; in 86 percent of schools, the gap between the lowest-performing and highest-performing one-fifth of students was equivalent to more than two years of schooling,[10] effectively creating multigrade classrooms.

FIGURE 1.5
**Variance of student outcomes between highest- and lowest-performing primary schools, 2016**

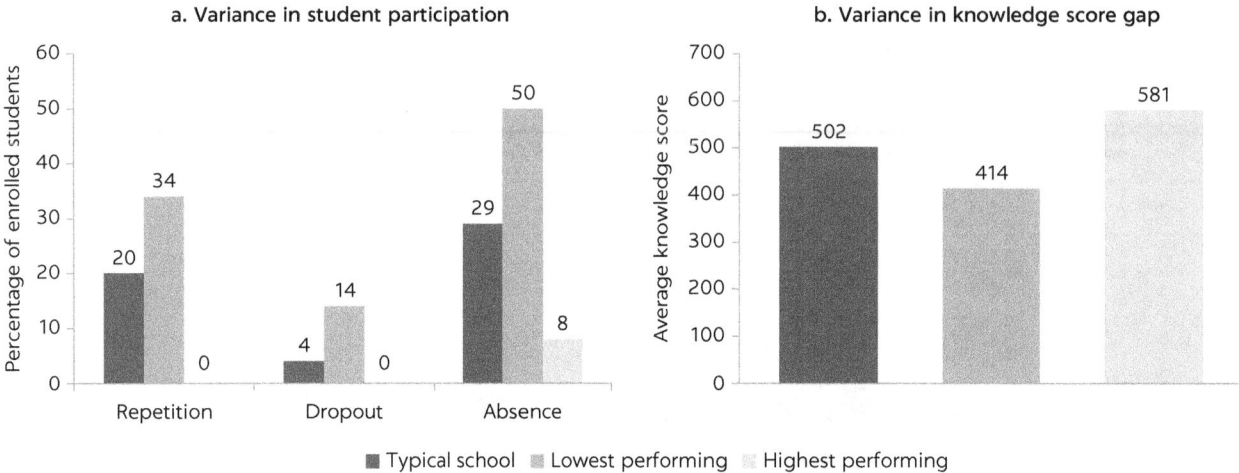

Source: World Bank calculations from Malawi Longitudinal School Survey baseline (2016) data.
Note: "Typical" refers to the median. "Lowest performing" designates the 90th percentile in dropout, repetition, and absenteeism rates or the 10th percentile in learning outcomes. "Highest performing" designates the 10th percentile in dropout, repetition, and absenteeism rates or the 90th percentile for learning outcomes.

FIGURE 1.6
**Variance of student knowledge scores, by subject, 2016**

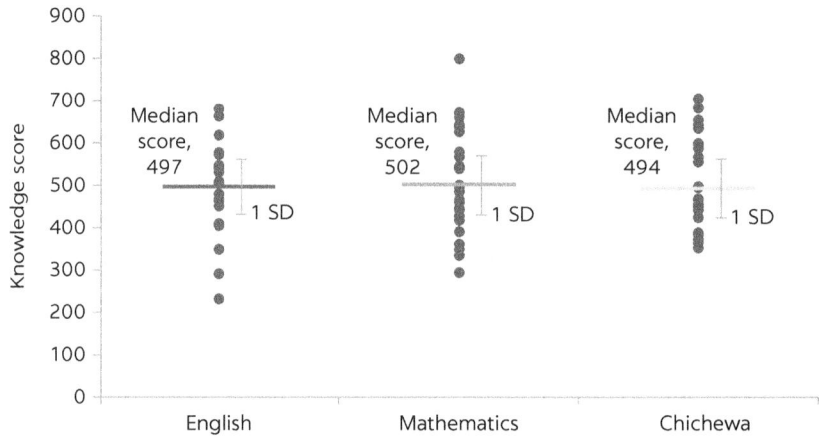

Source: World Bank calculations from Malawi Longitudinal School Survey baseline (2016) data.
Note: The figure depicts the distribution of student scores in a typical (median) rural school, by subject. Each dot represents one fourth-grade pupil at this median school. SD = standard deviation.

These low efficiencies and learning outcomes mean that Malawi performs poorly on the Human Capital Index (HCI). The HCI, developed by the World Bank, measures the human capital that a child born today can expect to attain by the child's 18th birthday (on a scale of 0–1). Malawi's index is 0.41, below those of the Republic of Congo, Gabon, Namibia, Togo, and Zimbabwe, among others. The HCI includes a measure of learning-adjusted years of schooling, which adjusts actual average years of school attainment in a country to account for levels of learning taking place. A child born today in Malawi can expect just

5.4 learning-adjusted years of schooling—less than in Benin, Cameroon, and Lesotho, among others.

## CONCLUSIONS: CHALLENGING MALAWI'S LOW-LEVEL EDUCATION EQUILIBRIUM

Malawi's primary education sector is stuck in a low-level equilibrium, with apparent high rates of access belied by high rates of absence and dropout. Those students who do progress learn little, and student learning levels vary enormously within a single class. These weaknesses reflect policy making based on national- and district-level average inputs, informed by education management information systems and other administrative data sources. The MLSS data enable more detailed analysis of the precise school, teacher, and student characteristics associated with poor learning outcomes. The following chapters present those insights and highlight opportunities for reforms.

## ANNEX 1A SUMMARY STATISTICS ON LEARNING OUTCOME DISPARITIES

TABLE 1A.1 **Performance indicators of student participation and learning outcomes in rural primary schools, 2016**

| PERFORMANCE INDICATORS | RURAL SCHOOLS (N = 504) | | | | | REMOTE SCHOOLS (n = 108) | | SCHOOLS CLOSE TO TC (n = 83) | |
|---|---|---|---|---|---|---|---|---|---|
| | MEAN | SD | P10 | P50 | P90 | MEAN | SD | MEAN | SD |
| Repetition rate (%, overall) | 20 | 12 | 0 | 20 | 34 | 20 | 13 | 20 | 13 |
| Grades 1–4, boys | 21 | 14 | 0 | 22 | 38 | 21 | 14 | 21 | 14 |
| Grades 1–4, girls | 20 | 13 | 0 | 20 | 36 | 20 | 13 | 19 | 13 |
| Grades 5–8, boys | 19 | 14 | 0 | 18 | 37 | 20 | 15 | 21 | 14 |
| Grades 5–8, girls | 19 | 15 | 0 | 17 | 36 | 18 | 15 | 20 | 14 |
| Dropout rate (%, overall) | 6 | 6 | 0 | 4 | 14 | 6 | 6 | 4 | 5 |
| Grades 1–4, boys | 6 | 7 | 0 | 4 | 14 | 5 | 8 | 5 | 6 |
| Grades 1–4, girls | 5 | 7 | 0 | 3 | 13 | 4 | 6 | 4 | 5 |
| Grades 5–8, boys | 6 | 8 | 0 | 4 | 15 | 6 | 8 | 5 | 6 |
| Grades 5–8, girls | 7 | 8 | 0 | 5 | 15 | 7 | 9 | 5 | 6 |
| Grade 8 survival rate (%, overall) | 26 | 16 | 8 | 21 | 49 | 25 | 14 | 33 | 21 |
| Grade 8 survival, boys | 27 | 17 | 9 | 22 | 52 | 25 | 15 | 35 | 20 |
| Grade 8 survival, girls | 24 | 18 | 6 | 20 | 50 | 26 | 18 | 32 | 23 |
| Grade 7 survival rate (%, overall) | 31 | 18 | 12 | 28 | 52 | 30 | 17 | 38 | 20 |
| Grade 7 survival, boys | 31 | 19 | 11 | 27 | 54 | 28 | 18 | 38 | 21 |
| Grade 7 survival, girls | 31 | 19 | 11 | 28 | 55 | 31 | 18 | 38 | 21 |
| Grade 4 survival rate (%, overall) | 50 | 20 | 25 | 48 | 77 | 51 | 19 | 55 | 20 |
| Grade 4 survival, boys | 49 | 22 | 21 | 46 | 79 | 49 | 21 | 56 | 21 |
| Grade 4 survival, girls | 52 | 22 | 25 | 50 | 83 | 54 | 22 | 54 | 20 |

*continued*

**TABLE 1A.1**, *continued*

| PERFORMANCE INDICATORS | RURAL SCHOOLS (N = 504) | | | | | REMOTE SCHOOLS (n = 108) | | SCHOOLS CLOSE TO TC (n = 83) | |
|---|---|---|---|---|---|---|---|---|---|
| | MEAN | SD | P10 | P50 | P90 | MEAN | SD | MEAN | SD |
| Student absence rate (%) | | | | | | | | | |
|   Record | 30 | 17 | 09 | 29 | 50 | 27 | 19 | 28 | 14 |
|   Headcount | 41 | 19 | 15 | 43 | 65 | 40 | 20 | 35 | 19 |
| Knowledge scores (overall) | 503 | 63 | 414 | 506 | 581 | 478 | 65 | 521 | 61 |
|   English | 499 | 59 | 426 | 502 | 579 | 478 | 65 | 521 | 61 |
|     Boys | 509 | 64 | 425 | 510 | 591 | 490 | 59 | 531 | 67 |
|     Girls | 490 | 67 | 403 | 488 | 574 | 468 | 69 | 516 | 68 |
|   Mathematics | 503 | 67 | 411 | 509 | 588 | 479 | 71 | 520 | 64 |
|     Boys | 516 | 73 | 419 | 521 | 612 | 491 | 73 | 534 | 68 |
|     Girls | 491 | 74 | 393 | 496 | 590 | 468 | 80 | 507 | 71 |
|   Chichewa | 505 | 71 | 408 | 508 | 592 | 478 | 72 | 520 | 67 |
|     Boys | 511 | 75 | 414 | 512 | 614 | 483 | 73 | 525 | 69 |
|     Girls | 500 | 79 | 394 | 505 | 596 | 473 | 81 | 517 | 78 |

*Source:* World Bank calculations from Malawi Longitudinal School Survey baseline (2016) data.
*Note:* Repetition rate is the share of repeaters of enrollment averaged across grades 1–8. Dropout rate is the share of enrolled students who drop out each year, averaged across grades 1–4 or 5–8. Survival rate of a certain grade is the percentage of grade 1 enrolled students who are expected to reach a certain grade, regardless of repetition. Summary statistics and regressions include data from rural schools only; 5 schools with missing data are not included. "Remote" is defined as being at the top quintile of distance (at least 9 km) from the nearest TC; "close to TC" is defined as being at the bottom quintile of distance (less than 2.9 km), with quintiles defined against a larger sample including urban schools. P10 = 10th percentile; P50 = 50th percentile; P90 = 90th percentile; SD = standard deviation; TC = trading center.

## NOTES

1. Of the Malawian primary schools in the MLSS baseline sample, only 11.1 percent met the national PCR goal of 60 to 1 in grade 1.
2. Twenty-six percent of classrooms have walls that are cracked or damaged; 8 percent have walls that are broken; and 56 percent have a floor that is uneven, is cracked, or has holes.
3. Throughout this report, "typical" refers to the median.
4. The gross enrollment ratio is the total number of students *enrolled* in a level of education divided by the population of the age group *intended* to attend that level of education. This ratio can exceed 100 percent in the event of under- or over-age enrollment.
5. The repetition rates are from 2017 "Repetition rate in primary education" data, United Nations Educational, Scientific and Cultural Organization Institute of Statistics, http://data.uis.unesco.org/.
6. Of the fourth-grade students, 14 percent achieved a score of zero on grade 1 mathematics tasks, 16 percent on grade 1 English tasks, and 15 percent on grade 1 Chichewa tasks.
7. Whereas on average, sampled students had a composite knowledge score of 502, in the top 10 percent of schools, the average was 581 or above; in the bottom 10 percent of schools, the average was below 414. This gap is equivalent to about three years' learning.
8. The largest range is in Chichewa, where 10 percent of schools have an average score of 591 or above and 10 percent a score of 408 or below, a delta of 183 points. For mathematics, the delta is 178 points and for English, 153 points.
9. In the Southern and Eastern Africa Consortium for Monitoring Educational Quality III 2007 and Programme for the Analysis of Education Systems 2014 assessments, the level of within-school variation in Malawi was greater than that in 19 of 26 countries for reading and 17 of 26 countries for mathematics (Bashir et al. 2018).
10. The gap in 86 percent of schools was at least 115 points, equivalent to about two years' schooling.

## REFERENCES

Bashir, S., M. Lockheed, E. Ninan, and J. Tan. 2018. *Facing Forward: Schooling for Learning in Africa*. Washington, DC: World Bank.

Bergmann, H. 1996. "Quality of Education and the Demands for Education: Evidence From Developing Countries." *International Review Of Education* 42 (6): 583–90.

Tran, L., and L. Gershenson. 2021. "Experimental Estimates of the Student Attendance Production Function." *Education Evaluation and Policy Analysis* 43 (2): 183–99.

World Bank. 2019. "International Development Association Project Appraisal Document on a Proposed Grant in the Amount of SDR 64/8 Million (US$90 Million Equivalent) to the Republic of Malawi for the Equity with Quality and Learning at Secondary Project (EQUALS)." Report No. PAD2918, World Bank, Washington, DC.

# 2 Schools

*LEARNING DISADVANTAGES IN REMOTE SCHOOLS*

**KEY POINTS**

Baseline data from the Malawi Longitudinal School Survey (MLSS)[1] reveal significant inequities in conditions between remote schools and schools close to trading centers—towns, large villages, or marketplaces. These inequities contribute to large variations in learning outcomes: students of similar ability and born within the same subdistrict may face strongly divergent learning trajectories as a result of which school they attend. However, new reforms have begun to address these disparities.

**CONSTRAINTS IN LEARNING CONDITIONS AT THE TYPICAL SCHOOL**

The typical Malawian primary school faces significant constraints in learning conditions.[2] As described in chapter 1, the typical school lacks electricity and has limited washing and hygiene facilities (refer to annex 2A, table 2A.1), with more than half of classrooms needing repair. A large minority of schools lack basic amenities: about a quarter of schools lose access by road during the rainy season, and almost a quarter (23 percent) of schools have no source of drinking water.[3]

Within the classroom, the typical school lacks basic learning materials, with three students sharing a textbook, only 40 percent of students seated on a chair (the remainder on the floor), and only 43 percent with a uniform. These poor conditions are concentrated in lower grades: on average, 18 percent of students sit on a chair in grade 1, 49 percent in grade 5, and 90 percent in grade 8.[4] More than half the grade 1–2 classrooms observed had zero textbooks in use, a share that falls to one-fifth in grades 7–8.[5]

## INEQUITIES IN CONDITIONS BETWEEN REMOTE SCHOOLS AND THOSE NEAR TRADING CENTERS

### Inequities in school amenities, condition, and supplies

There are enormous inequities in learning environments between remote schools and those close to trading centers. We define "remote schools" as the 20 percent of MLSS schools farthest from the nearest trading center (at least 9 kilometers away). The 20 percent of schools closest to trading centers (less than 2.9 kilometers from the nearest trading center) are defined as "schools close to a trading center." The MLSS analysis uses an official classification of more than 200 trading centers used by the National Statistical Office of Malawi. We measure the distance from a school to the nearest trading center using a geographic database developed from administrative data (Asim et al. 2019).

Remote schools face significant limitations as a direct result of their location; they are less likely to be connected to a properly constructed road than schools close to a trading center and, as a result, three times as likely to become inaccessible by road during the rainy season.[6] Remote schools are also more likely to lack electricity and handwashing facilities.[7] In addition to these unequal endowments, however, remote schools also appear to face significant inequities in infrastructure and resources, financing, staffing, and supervision.

Remote schools are more likely to need repairs to their classrooms and to lack basic teaching and learning materials. Although remote schools do not face significantly greater shortages of classrooms[8] or student learning materials (SLM), such as pens and pencils, notebooks, textbooks, and chairs,[9] than do those close to a trading center; their classrooms are significantly more likely to be in need of repair;[10] and they are more likely to lack basic teaching and learning materials (such as a blackboard, chalk, or a chair for the teacher) (refer to figure 2.1).[11]

**FIGURE 2.1**

**Comparison of infrastructure and materials in remote schools versus those near TCs, 2016**

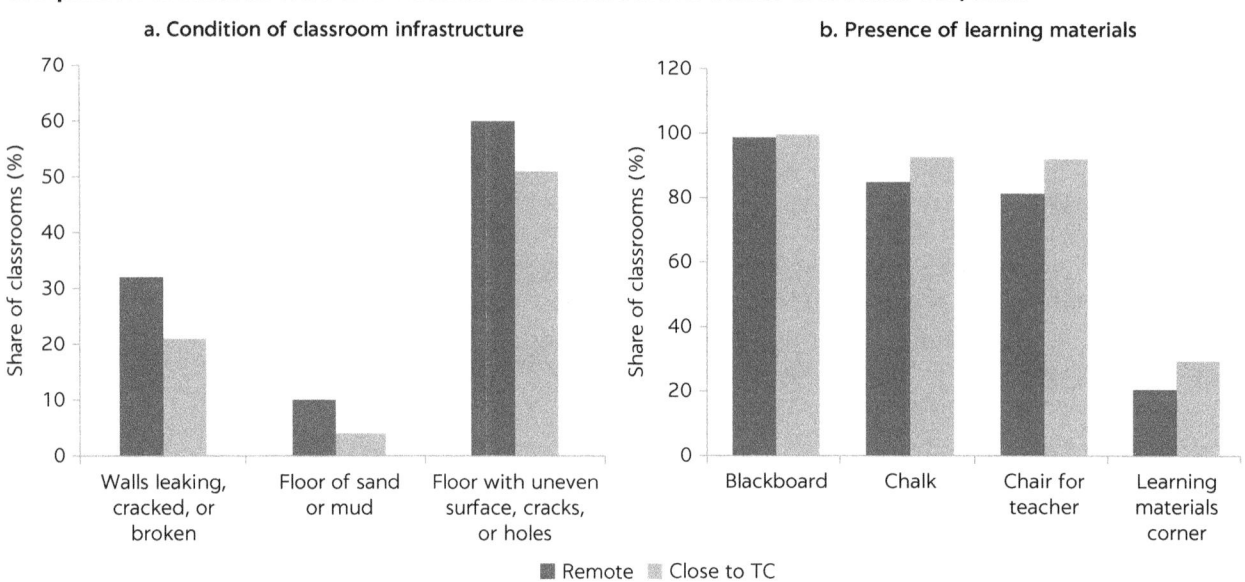

*Source:* Malawi Longitudinal School Survey (MLSS) baseline (2016) data.
*Note:* Data include both urban and rural schools. TC = trading center.

Our two MLSS case study schools illustrate this difference. Kamulindeni primary school is 7 kilometers from the heart of the Mabulabo trading center. In all of its seven classrooms, the walls, floors, and roofs are in fine condition, although two have cracked windows. On average, 1.9 students share a textbook, and 84 percent of the students wear a uniform. By contrast, Chamkoko school is 13 kilometers from Mabulabo. Three of its seven classrooms have cracked walls, and one has walls that are severely broken. Six classrooms have cracked floors. Four students share a textbook on average, and only 11 percent of the students wear a uniform.

### Inequities in school financing

**School financing is not designed to meet the needs of remote schools.** In the MLSS baseline data, although per-student levels of the School Improvement Grants (SIGs) are not significantly lower in remote schools,[12] the needs-based component of SIGs accounts for less than 15 percent of overall grant financing—an inadequate amount to address these disparities in learning environments. Furthermore, delays in SIG receipt are more common in remote schools, which in 2014/15 received SIGs an average of 24 days later than schools close to a trading center.[13]

**Remote schools are more likely to divert SIG financing to address staffing shortages.** Remote schools are less likely to invest SIGs in classrooms, learning environments, and training, but they are more likely to invest to address shortages of staffing (refer to box 2.1), either in teacher salaries or

---

**BOX 2.1**

### Inequitable teacher distribution between remote schools and schools near trading centers

Malawi's education system has made considerable strides in recent years in addressing systemic shortages of teachers, reducing the national pupil-teacher ratio (PTR) from 70 pupils per teacher to 61 from 2014 to 2023 through large-scale deployment of newly qualified teachers (MoEST 2014; MoE 2023) However, the Malawian system is failing to achieve an efficient distribution of teachers between schools. Nationally, the best-staffed 10 percent of schools have a PTR below 39—well below the national target—but 20 percent have a PTR above 90 pupils per teacher, according to the Malawi Longitudinal School Survey (MLSS) baseline data.

This variation occurs on a microgeographic scale, with PTRs varying by an average of five times within a single zone. About 40 percent of variation in teacher numbers within a district is unexplained by differences in school enrollment, a greater level than in Lesotho, South Africa, Tanzania, and Zimbabwe (Bashir et al. 2018).

**Significantly higher PTRs in remote schools**

The average remote school has 91 pupils for each qualified teacher versus 68 in schools close to a trading center. Remote schools are 30 percent more likely than schools close to a trading center to have a school PTR above the national standard of 60 to 1. These disparities reflect the weaknesses of Malawi's systems for the allocation of teachers to schools and incentives for teachers in remote postings (Asim et al. 2019). These inequities interact with underallocation of teachers to lower-primary grades (as discussed in chapter 3) to create extremely large class sizes in lower grades in remote schools.

*continued*

Box 2.1, continued

**Particularly poor distribution of female teachers**

The teaching workforce at MLSS baseline schools is 47 percent female. However, more than one-third (37 percent) of female teachers are clustered together in the 20 percent of schools close to a trading center. Only 1 in 10 female teachers is based in a remote school. The result is that the typical school has only one female teacher for every 97 female students versus one male teacher for every 51 male students, and 12 percent of schools have no female teachers at all.

This situation leaves female students, particularly in remote schools, without role models who are more likely to encourage and empower their learning. These problems are particularly acute in upper grades, which are also prone to shortages of female teachers. In remote schools, on average, there are 163 female students for every female teacher in upper primary. These shortages may contribute to higher rates of female dropout in upper grades.

**Disproportionate shares of junior teachers and higher teacher absence in remote schools**

Remote schools also tend to have less experienced teachers. We rank schools by the proportion of their teachers who are at level PT4, the most junior: 24 percent of remote schools are in the top fifth of schools by share of PT4 teachers versus just 19 percent of schools close to a trading center. Teachers in remote schools are also twice as likely to fail to arrive to conduct a lesson than those in schools close to a trading center. In 13 percent of the scheduled lessons observed in remote schools, the teacher never arrived to conduct the lesson. This was the case in just 5 percent of observed lessons in schools close to a trading center.

Our case study schools provide a clear example of how staff profiles vary between more and less remote schools. At Kamulindeni, 7 kilometers from the trading center, five out seven teachers are female, and the school has one female teacher for every 35 female students. At Chamkoko, 6 kilometers farther from the trading center, two out of five teachers are female, and the ratio of female students to female teachers is 109 to 1. Three out of seven (43 percent) of Kamulindeni's teachers are junior PT4 teachers versus three out of five (60 percent) of Chamkoko's.

**Disparities' impact on learning**

A regression analysis of the teacher characteristics associated with learning in the MLSS learning assessments confirms that disparities in teacher populations between schools have significant impacts on learning (refer to annex 2A, table 2A.3, panels b and c). Schools with a PTR above 90 to 1 achieve lower learning outcomes, as do those that rely heavily on junior (PT4) teachers and those with a higher share of teachers from the same district as the school. The findings suggest an urgent need to recalibrate teacher allocation policies and procedures to ensure all schools have adequate staffing.

housing (refer to figure 2.2). The average remote school spent four times as much of its SIG on teacher salaries in 2015/16 as on classroom construction. As a result of these disparities, the average remote school has less than half as much available in its bank account (MK 62,000, or US$84) as the average school close to a trading center (MK 196,000, or US$265).

### Inequities in supervision and staffing

Official systems of supervision are more effective for schools close to a trading center. Primary Education Advisers, subdistrict-level education officers, are expected to visit schools at least once per term to provide support and guidance to teachers and school leadership. Schools close to a trading center received an average of 4.2 such visits in 2015/16, significantly more than remote schools, which received an average of 3.2 visits. Schools are also supposed to receive annual visits from inspectors and occasional visits from

#### FIGURE 2.2
**Comparison of SIG investments in remote schools versus those near TCs, by category, 2016**

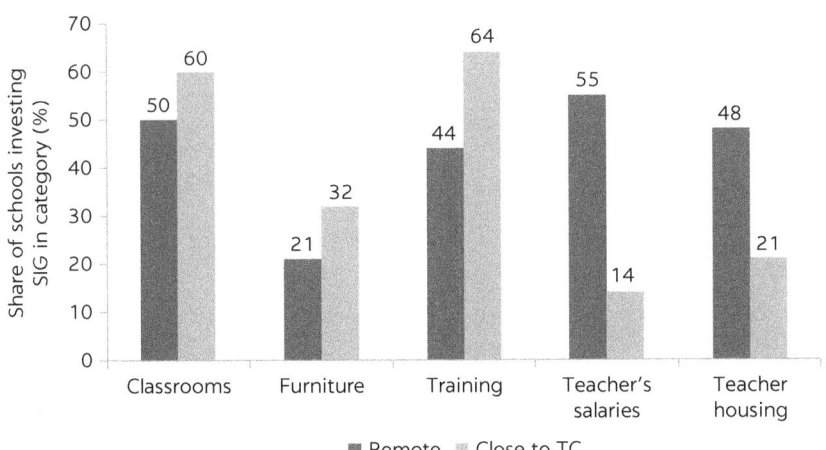

*Source:* Malawi Longitudinal School Survey baseline (2016) data.
*Note:* Data include both rural and urban schools. SIG = School Improvement Grant; TC = trading center.

District Education Managers (known in some districts as Chief Education Officers or Directors of Education, Youth and Sports). Remote schools were only about one-third as likely as schools close to a trading center to be visited by an inspector or District Education Manager.[14]

## POORER STUDENT OUTCOMES AT REMOTE SCHOOLS THAN AT THOSE NEAR TRADING CENTERS

As a result of these and other disparities, remote schools have significantly worse outputs—and learning outcomes—than those closer to trading centers (as shown in chapter 1, annex 1A, table 1A.1). Across grades, remote schools have higher dropout rates (refer to figure 2.3).

#### FIGURE 2.3
**Dropout rates in remote schools versus those near TCs, by grade, 2016**

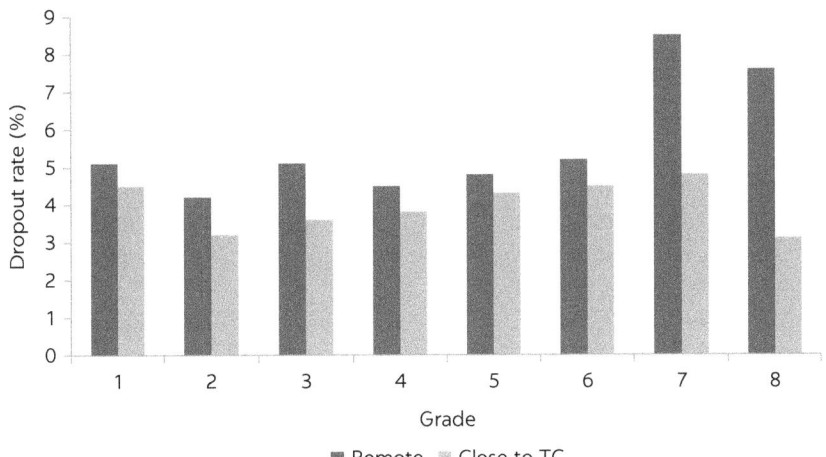

*Source:* Malawi Longitudinal School Survey baseline (2016) data.
*Note:* TC = trading center.

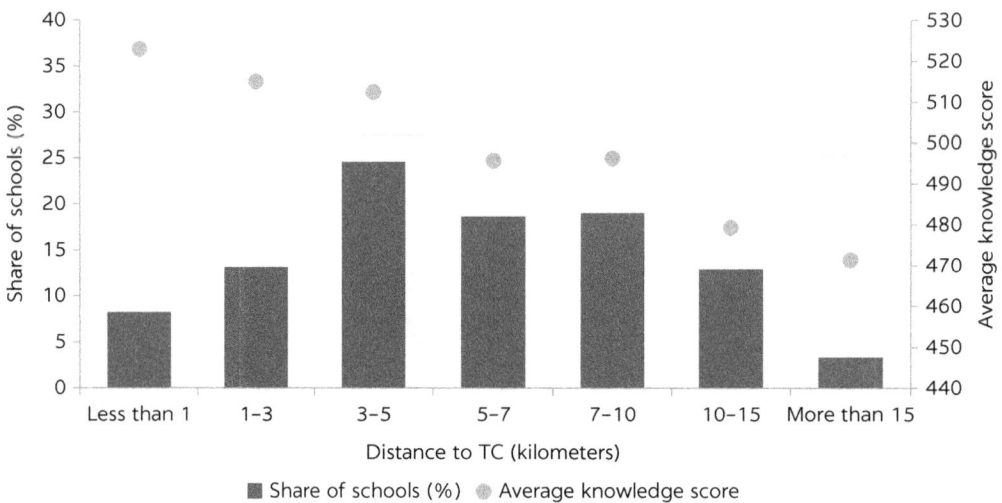

FIGURE 2.4

**Knowledge scores, by distance from TC, 2016**

*Source:* Malawi Longitudinal School Survey baseline (2016) data.
*Note:* TC = trading center.

Across subjects, grade 4 students in remote schools have lower learning outcomes than students in schools close to trading centers, a gap equivalent to about nine months' learning.[15] Average scores reduce consistently for every additional kilometer of distance between a school and the nearest trading center (refer to figure 2.4).

## WHAT MATTERS FOR LEARNING?

To what extent do the variations in inputs, conditions, financing, and supervision between more and less remote schools explain these disparities in learning? We conduct regression analysis to identify the impacts of school characteristics on learning (refer to annex 2A, table 2A.3, panel c).[16] Our analysis includes controls for a range of school conditions, including staffing and student characteristics, and for students' innate intelligence.[17]

**Teacher staffing and distribution.** Shortages of teachers have strong negative impacts on learning. Schools with a PTR above 90 to 1, suggesting severe shortages of staff, have average scores 13 points below those with lower PTRs. This effect persists even when controlling for remoteness, despite the fact that PTRs are highest in remote schools (as discussed in box 2.1). The finding confirms that the poor distribution of teachers between Malawi's schools has negative impacts on learning for students in the most understaffed schools.

**Adequate SLM.** Schools with fewer desks, notebooks, and uniforms achieve scores significantly below those of schools that are better equipped. An increase of 1 standard deviation increase in SLM is associated with an increase of 7 points in average learning outcomes across subjects.[18] However, unlike many other inputs, student learning materials are not consistently less available in remote schools.

**Proximity to a trading center.** Remoteness appears to have a powerful impact on learning outcomes, even controlling for other factors. Even with a wide range of school characteristics included in the regression—including availability of drinking water and electricity, condition of infrastructure, and availability of teaching and learning materials as well as a range of teacher and student characteristics—the distance from a school to the nearest trading center remains a strong (although not statistically significant) source of variation in learning outcomes.

The addition of 10 kilometers' distance from the nearest trading center is associated with a reduction in learning outcomes of 14 points, equivalent to several weeks' learning. This finding suggests that, in addition to the inequities in learning environments described earlier, additional unobserved factors, correlated with distance, negatively affect student learning outcomes. These factors may include costs to students from residing in remote areas, such as time spent supporting families in basic tasks, like shopping for necessities, which constitute significant time commitments in these areas.

## CONCLUSIONS: INEQUITIES IN SCHOOL CONDITIONS AND LEARNING BASED ON LOCATION

The MLSS findings show significant inequities between Malawi's primary schools in terms of conditions and resources. Schools farther from trading centers have classrooms in poorer condition, and are more likely to lack adequate teaching and learning materials, than those close to trading centers. Remote schools also receive fewer visits from inspectors and education officials. The poor condition of classrooms and facilities at remote schools demonstrates the need for school financing to provide additional support to remote schools to address these challenges. Furthermore, remote schools appear to divert significant portions of discretionary funding to address gaps in staffing, both by hiring auxiliary teachers from school funds and by investing substantial amounts in teacher housing.

These disparities in inputs have measurable impacts on learning: remote schools have significantly lower learning outcomes, and higher rates of student dropout, than those close to trading centers.

With the MLSS data's high-resolution picture of school-level inequities, new policies will target the needs of remote and overcrowded schools. Building on the MLSS data, the Malawi Education Reform Program introduces revisions to the needs-based component of SIGs to provide additional support to remote schools and includes targeted support for teachers who teach in these schools (as noted in box I.1 in the introduction to this report).[19] The Malawi Education Reform Program also provides targeted support for classroom construction at severely overcrowded schools.

## ANNEX 2A STATISTICAL AND REGRESSION TABLES

TABLE 2A.1 **Summary statistics on grade 1-8 school conditions and facilities, 2016**

| CHARACTERISTIC | ALL RURAL SCHOOLS (N = 504) | | | | | REMOTE SCHOOLS (n = 108) | | SCHOOLS CLOSE TO TC (n = 83) | |
|---|---|---|---|---|---|---|---|---|---|
| | MEAN | SD | P10 | P50 | P90 | MEAN | SD | MEAN | SD |
| Religious school (%) | 48 | 50 | 0 | 0 | 100 | 50 | 50 | 55 | 50 |
| Distance to nearest trading center (km) | 6.17 | 4.24 | 1.44 | 5.39 | 11.26 | 12.34 | 3.84 | 1.12 | 0.74 |
| School has electricity available (%) | 16 | 37 | 0 | 0 | 100 | 12 | 33 | 30 | 46 |
| School has drinking water available (%) | 77 | 42 | 0 | 100 | .00 | 74 | 44 | 77 | 42 |
| School has access to road during rainy seasons (%) | 73 | 44 | 0 | 100 | 100 | 72 | 45 | 93 | 26 |
| IQI[a] | −0.15 | 1.52 | −2.27 | 0.18 | 1.42 | −0.14 | 1.31 | 0.19 | 1.26 |
| TLM index[b] | 0 | 0.93 | −1.14 | 0.38 | 0.63 | −0.19 | 1.06 | 0.28 | 0.62 |
| Classrooms with learning corners (%) | 22 | 31 | 0 | 0 | 50 | 20 | 30 | 30 | 33 |
| Classrooms with blackboards (%) | 98 | 9 | 100 | 100 | 100 | 98 | 10 | 100 | 0 |
| Classrooms with chalk (%) | 89 | 23 | 50 | 100 | 100 | 87 | 25 | 92 | 20 |
| Classrooms with chairs or desks for the teacher to sit (%) | 86 | 26 | 50 | 100 | 100 | 79 | 29 | 94 | 19 |
| SLM index[c] | 0.05 | 1.07 | −1.90 | 0.29 | 1.53 | −0.05 | 1.11 | 0.07 | 1.09 |
|    Students with pen or pencils and notebooks (%) | 91 | 11 | 79 | 95 | 100 | 91 | 9 | 92 | 10 |
|    Students with chairs or desks (%) | 44 | 30 | 5 | 40 | 94 | 44 | 30 | 41 | 29 |
|    Students with uniforms (%) | 45 | 24 | 15 | 43 | 79 | 43 | 24 | 47 | 25 |
|    Pupil-textbook ratio | 3.96 | 4.74 | 1.25 | 2.75 | 7.44 | 3.77 | 3.08 | 4.38 | 5.04 |
| Classrooms with children's work displayed on the walls (%) | 39 | 28 | 0 | 33 | 80 | 32 | 27 | 46 | 31 |
| Classrooms where date on the board is today's date (%) | 68 | 24 | 33 | 71 | 100 | 65 | 27 | 72 | 20 |
| Classrooms with instructional materials posted on the walls (%) | 56 | 30 | 14 | 57 | 100 | 49 | 30 | 63 | 30 |
| Classrooms with teacher present (%) | 67 | 25 | 29 | 71 | 100 | 61 | 24 | 79 | 21 |
| School PTR above 90 to 1 (%) | 20 | 40 | 0 | 0 | 100 | 27 | 44 | 13 | 33 |
| Total enrollment | 873 | 575 | 283 | 738 | 1,623 | 692 | 384 | 1,259 | 778 |
| Number of classroom blocks in school | 4.51 | 2.25 | 2.00 | 4.00 | 7.00 | 3.95 | 1.73 | 5.79 | 2.71 |
| Number of teacher housing units in school | 4.89 | 2.98 | 1.00 | 5.00 | 9.00 | 5.42 | 2.81 | 5.61 | 3.80 |

*continued*

TABLE 2A.1, continued

| CHARACTERISTIC | ALL RURAL SCHOOLS (N = 504) | | | | | REMOTE SCHOOLS (n = 108) | | SCHOOLS CLOSE TO TC (n = 83) | |
|---|---|---|---|---|---|---|---|---|---|
| | MEAN | SD | P10 | P50 | P90 | MEAN | SD | MEAN | SD |
| Share of students with 1+ years of pre-primary education (%) | 66 | 32 | 24 | 68 | 100 | 53 | 31 | 77 | 29 |
| School lacks female leadership position (%) | 44 | 50 | 0 | 0 | 100 | 64 | 48 | 37 | 48 |
| Class size in grade 1 is above 100 (enrollment) (%) | 72 | 45 | 0 | 100 | 100 | 65 | 48 | 74 | 44 |
| School average overall score | 503 | 63 | 414 | 506 | 581 | 478 | 65 | 521 | 61 |
| School average English score | 499 | 59 | 426 | 502 | 579 | 478 | 59 | 524 | 60 |
| School average math score | 503 | 67 | 411 | 509 | 590 | 479 | 72 | 520 | 64 |
| School average Chichewa score | 505 | 71 | 408 | 508 | 592 | 478 | 72 | 520 | 67 |

Source: Malawi Longitudinal School Survey baseline (2016) data.
Note: See table 1A.1 for details of included schools. IQI = infrastructure quality index; P10 = 10th percentile; P50 = 50th percentile; P90 = 90th percentile; PTR = pupil-teacher ratio; SD = standard deviation; SLM = student learning materials; TLM = teaching and learning materials.
a. The IQI is a principal component analysis (PCA) index assigned to each school based on the use of open-air classrooms and the materials and condition of walls, roofs, floors, windows, and doors in classrooms.
b. The TLM index is a PCA index constructed at the classroom level from binary items based on whether classroom has a blackboard, chalk, a chair or desk for the teacher, or a learning materials corner. Index is averaged at the school level.
c. The SLM index is a PCA index constructed from dichotomic items using the following thresholds: share of students with pen or pencil or notebook above the median; share of students with uniforms above the median; pupil-desk ratio of 3 to 1 or above; and pupil-textbook ratio of 4 to 1 or above.

TABLE 2A.2 **Summary statistics on school finances and expenditures, 2016**
*Malawian kwacha (MK)*

| FINANCES AND EXPENDITURES | TOTAL (N = 556) | | | | | REMOTE SCHOOLS (n = 120) | | SCHOOLS CLOSE TO TC (n = 107) | |
|---|---|---|---|---|---|---|---|---|---|
| | MEAN | SD | P10 | P50 | P90 | MEAN | SD | MEAN | SD |
| a. Finances (cash and in-kind) | | | | | | | | | |
| School Improvement Grant | | | | | | | | | |
| Amount, 2015 | 677,601 | 307,409 | 40,000 | 700,000 | 967,087 | 650,811 | 332,008 | 767,560 | 353,718 |
| Amount, 2016 | 618,642 | 329,342 | 0 | 674,000 | 948,000 | 563,218 | 319,451 | 716,987 | 390,166 |
| Balance, 2016 | 151,515 | 421,566 | 0 | 13,173 | 500,000 | 67,114 | 149,676 | 186,138 | 330,199 |
| Community contributions (cash) | | | | | | | | | |
| Amount, 2015 | 110,682 | 122,811 | 10,000 | 72,000 | 274,042 | 85,680 | 101,816 | 175,546 | 152,158 |
| Amount, 2016 | 122,778 | 167,618 | 8,255 | 59,000 | 320,000 | 81,044 | 133,622 | 219,797 | 236,562 |
| Community contributions (in-kind) | | | | | | | | | |
| Desks and chairs, 2015 | 458 | 2,635 | 32 | 60 | 237 | 111 | 84 | 1,418 | 5,046 |
| Desks and chairs, 2016 | 71 | 56 | 20 | 51 | 120 | 62 | 38 | 82 | 67 |
| Exercises/notebooks, 2015 | 1,104 | 1,248 | 80 | 680 | 3,120 | 655 | 598 | 815 | 639 |
| Exercises/notebooks, 2016 | 1,719 | 2,561 | 30 | 530 | 5,000 | 595 | 377 | 1,378 | 1,806 |
| Labor man-days, 2015 | 65 | 56 | 4 | 45 | 150 | 67 | 63 | 58 | 54 |
| Labor man-days, 2016 | 48 | 48 | 4 | 28 | 120 | 44 | 55 | 48 | 44 |

*continued*

TABLE 2A.2, *continued*

| FINANCES AND EXPENDITURES | TOTAL (N = 556) | | | | | REMOTE SCHOOLS (n = 120) | | SCHOOLS CLOSE TO TC (n = 107) | |
|---|---|---|---|---|---|---|---|---|---|
| | MEAN | SD | P10 | P50 | P90 | MEAN | SD | MEAN | SD |
| *b. Expenditures* | | | | | | | | | |
| Classroom | | | | | | | | | |
| Repairs/construction, 2016 | 160,359 | 162,756 | 20,600 | 135,250 | 306,496 | 173,048 | 147,953 | 162,328 | 125,790 |
| Fixtures and fittings, 2016 | 30,652 | 46,300 | 1,500 | 15,000 | 100,000 | 26,600 | 40,609 | 65,850 | 87,484 |
| TLM, 2016 | 215,758 | 119,527 | 57,000 | 208,350 | 375,617 | 177,040 | 101,059 | 230,617 | 146,150 |
| Teachers | | | | | | | | | |
| Auxiliary, 2016 | 107,786 | 67,182 | 20,000 | 100,000 | 204,000 | 109,597 | 63,462 | 96,675 | 70,193 |
| Housing, 2016 | 134,481 | 132,169 | 18,600 | 100,400 | 280,000 | 122,784 | 130,182 | 109,426 | 95,203 |

*Source:* Malawi Longitudinal School Survey (2016) data.
*Note:* The table shows data for rural and urban schools (N = 559), of which 3 schools with incomplete data are not included. Of 559 schools, 120 schools are "remote," and 109 are "close to TC." P10 = 10th percentile; P50 = 50th percentile; P90 = 90th percentile; SD = standard deviation; TLM = teaching and learning materials.

TABLE 2A.3 **Regression analysis of school-level factors' impacts on grade 4 learning outcomes**

| CHARACTERISTIC | WITH CHARACTERISTICS ESTIMATED AT SCHOOL LEVEL | | | | WITH ADDITION OF INDIVIDUAL STUDENT CHARACTERISTICS | | | |
|---|---|---|---|---|---|---|---|---|
| | OVERALL | ENGLISH | MATH | CHICHEWA | OVERALL | ENGLISH | MATH | CHICHEWA |
| *a. Students' characteristics (aggregated at L2)* | | | | | | | | |
| Students above median age[a,c] | 7.66*** | 5.38*** | 9.21*** | 8.42*** | 8.90*** | 6.84*** | 9.88*** | 9.98*** |
| | (1.50) | (1.45) | (1.62) | (1.69) | (1.51) | (1.47) | (1.64) | (1.70) |
| Female students[a,c] | 3.56 | 3.91 | 2.05 | 5.02 | 4.98 | 5.51 | 4.02 | 5.70 |
| | (4.48) | (4.35) | (4.85) | (5.04) | (4.48) | (4.35) | (4.85) | (5.03) |
| Students above median SES[a,c] | 1.23 | 2.97** | 0.31 | 0.38 | 0.88 | 2.13 | −0.03 | 0.44 |
| | (1.46) | (1.42) | (1.58) | (1.64) | (1.48) | (1.44) | (1.61) | (1.66) |
| Students having at least one literate parent[a,c] | 5.47** | 4.41** | 5.48** | 6.53*** | 5.26** | 4.50** | 5.07** | 6.27*** |
| | (2.14) | (2.07) | (2.31) | (2.40) | (2.15) | (2.09) | (2.33) | (2.42) |
| Students speaking Chichewa at home[a,c] | 5.19*** | 4.19*** | 5.21*** | 6.18*** | 4.91*** | 3.99*** | 4.54*** | 6.16*** |
| | (1.44) | (1.39) | (1.56) | (1.62) | (1.48) | (1.45) | (1.62) | (1.67) |
| Students receiving help from parents on homework at home[a] | 3.22** | 2.85* | 3.28** | 3.57** | 3.75** | 3.45** | 3.58** | 4.31** |
| | (1.54) | (1.49) | (1.66) | (1.73) | (1.55) | (1.51) | (1.68) | (1.75) |
| Students were absent on any day last week[a,c] | −6.14*** | −5.07*** | −7.01*** | −6.31*** | −4.73*** | −3.78** | −5.64*** | −4.75** |
| | (1.73) | (1.68) | (1.87) | (1.95) | (1.74) | (1.69) | (1.89) | (1.96) |
| Raw Raven Test Score (0–6)[b] | 5.07 | 1.72 | 9.21 | 4.23 | −0.69 | −3.71 | 3.59 | −1.69 |
| | (5.38) | (5.20) | (5.81) | (6.04) | (5.47) | (5.32) | (5.93) | (6.15) |
| Students agree that "You are interested in talking to new kids in school" describes them[a,c] | 4.60** | 6.18*** | 2.32 | 5.37** | 3.00 | 4.87** | 0.39 | 3.68 |
| | (2.17) | (2.10) | (2.35) | (2.44) | (2.21) | (2.15) | (2.40) | (2.49) |

*continued*

TABLE 2A.3, continued

| CHARACTERISTIC | WITH CHARACTERISTICS ESTIMATED AT SCHOOL LEVEL | | | | WITH ADDITION OF INDIVIDUAL STUDENT CHARACTERISTICS | | | |
|---|---|---|---|---|---|---|---|---|
| | OVERALL | ENGLISH | MATH | CHICHEWA | OVERALL | ENGLISH | MATH | CHICHEWA |
| Students agree that "When you start my homework you tend to finish it" describes them[a,c] | 6.97*** | 4.80* | 9.80*** | 6.29** | 5.89** | 4.17 | 8.35*** | 5.28* |
| | (2.66) | (2.57) | (2.87) | (2.99) | (2.72) | (2.65) | (2.95) | (3.06) |
| Students agree that "Failing in a test frustrates you" describes them[a,c] | 7.67*** | 7.08*** | 7.43*** | 8.47*** | 6.95*** | 6.67*** | 6.29** | 7.96*** |
| | (2.52) | (2.43) | (2.72) | (2.83) | (2.54) | (2.47) | (2.75) | (2.85) |
| Students agree that "Teachers or parents often tell you that you are not performing to your potential" describes them | −1.81 | −1.44 | −2.45 | −1.53 | −1.06 | −0.76 | −1.92 | −0.51 |
| | (1.78) | (1.73) | (1.93) | (2.00) | (1.80) | (1.75) | (1.95) | (2.02) |
| *b. Teachers' characteristics (aggregated at L2)* | | | | | | | | |
| Age of teacher[b] | 0.14 | 0.75 | 0.34 | −0.67 | 0.12 | 0.72 | 0.34 | −0.69 |
| | (0.76) | (0.73) | (0.82) | (0.85) | (0.75) | (0.73) | (0.82) | (0.85) |
| Teacher is PT4 (student teacher or teacher assistant)[a,c] | −3.58** | −3.52** | −3.73** | −3.47* | −3.78** | −3.70** | −3.99** | −3.68* |
| | (1.72) | (1.66) | (1.86) | (1.93) | (1.72) | (1.67) | (1.86) | (1.93) |
| Teacher tenure at school (in years)[b] | −1.02 | −1.59 | −0.77 | −0.72 | −1.27 | −1.79 | −1.04 | −1.01 |
| | (1.41) | (1.37) | (1.52) | (1.59) | (1.41) | (1.37) | (1.53) | (1.58) |
| Teacher is from the same district as the school[a,c] | −3.29*** | −3.78*** | −3.22** | −2.85** | −3.24*** | −3.74*** | −3.14** | −2.83** |
| | (1.23) | (1.19) | (1.33) | (1.39) | (1.23) | (1.20) | (1.33) | (1.38) |
| Teacher commuting time to school in minutes[b] (per 10 min.) | −0.90 | 1.41 | −1.89 | −2.30 | −0.83 | 1.50 | −1.85 | −2.20 |
| | (2.66) | (2.58) | (2.88) | (2.99) | (2.66) | (2.58) | (2.88) | (2.99) |
| Number of salary delays in the last 12 months[b] | −6.22*** | −4.47** | −7.24*** | −6.94*** | −6.08*** | −4.36** | −7.12*** | −6.73*** |
| | (1.80) | (1.74) | (1.94) | (2.02) | (1.79) | (1.74) | (1.94) | (2.01) |
| Teacher content knowledge (English) in percentage points[b] | −1.08 | −1.27* | −0.90 | −1.05 | −1.12 | −1.31* | −0.94 | −1.10 |
| | (0.71) | (0.68) | (0.76) | (0.79) | (0.70) | (0.68) | (0.76) | (0.79) |
| Teacher content knowledge (mathematics) in percentage points[b] | 0.26 | 0.33 | 0.27 | 0.18 | 0.28 | 0.37 | 0.31 | 0.16 |
| | (0.53) | (0.51) | (0.57) | (0.59) | (0.53) | (0.51) | (0.57) | (0.59) |
| Teacher's performance is assessed[a,c] | −0.52 | −0.67 | −0.59 | −0.29 | −0.36 | −0.60 | −0.40 | −0.06 |
| | (1.35) | (1.31) | (1.46) | (1.52) | (1.35) | (1.31) | (1.46) | (1.52) |
| Teacher's performance is encouraged[a,c] | 1.22 | 1.74 | 0.87 | 1.06 | 1.21 | 1.76 | 0.83 | 1.03 |
| | (1.18) | (1.14) | (1.27) | (1.33) | (1.18) | (1.14) | (1.27) | (1.32) |
| Teacher is satisfied with the job[a,c] | −0.55 | −0.09 | −1.02 | −0.55 | −0.66 | −0.20 | −1.14 | −0.66 |
| | (1.30) | (1.26) | (1.40) | (1.46) | (1.30) | (1.26) | (1.41) | (1.46) |
| *c. School characteristics (L2)* | | | | | | | | |
| Religious school | −0.16 | −0.80 | 0.77 | −0.40 | 0.28 | −0.39 | 1.13 | 0.20 |
| | (4.60) | (4.45) | (4.97) | (5.17) | (4.60) | (4.46) | (4.97) | (5.16) |
| Distance to nearest trading center (in km) (per 10 km) | −8.85 | −8.36 | −7.99 | −10.23 | −8.55 | −8.20 | −7.72 | −9.76 |
| | (5.85) | (5.66) | (6.32) | (6.57) | (5.84) | (5.66) | (6.32) | (6.55) |
| School has electricity available | 3.98 | 7.95 | 3.61 | 0.38 | 3.16 | 7.12 | 2.66 | −0.52 |
| | (6.33) | (6.13) | (6.84) | (7.12) | (6.35) | (6.16) | (6.86) | (7.12) |

*continued*

TABLE 2A.3, *continued*

| CHARACTERISTIC | WITH CHARACTERISTICS ESTIMATED AT SCHOOL LEVEL | | | | WITH ADDITION OF INDIVIDUAL STUDENT CHARACTERISTICS | | | |
|---|---|---|---|---|---|---|---|---|
| | OVERALL | ENGLISH | MATH | CHICHEWA | OVERALL | ENGLISH | MATH | CHICHEWA |
| School has drinking water available | 5.56 | 3.34 | 7.81 | 5.61 | 5.29 | 3.11 | 7.45 | 5.37 |
| | (5.35) | (5.18) | (5.78) | (6.01) | (5.34) | (5.18) | (5.78) | (6.00) |
| School has access to road during rainy seasons | −7.96 | −6.42 | −8.43 | −8.97 | −7.41 | −6.09 | −7.69 | −8.37 |
| | (5.55) | (5.37) | (5.99) | (6.23) | (5.54) | (5.37) | (5.99) | (6.22) |
| IQI[d] | 1.21 | 0.87 | 1.42 | 1.31 | 1.48 | 1.04 | 1.72 | 1.65 |
| | (1.83) | (1.77) | (1.98) | (2.05) | (1.83) | (1.77) | (1.98) | (2.05) |
| TLM index[e] | −1.81 | −0.11 | −3.32 | −1.93 | −1.80 | −0.04 | −3.49 | −1.85 |
| | (2.80) | (2.71) | (3.02) | (3.14) | (2.80) | (2.71) | (3.03) | (3.14) |
| SLM index[f] | 5.62** | 6.23*** | 4.13* | 6.49*** | 5.19** | 5.83*** | 3.70 | 6.00** |
| | (2.18) | (2.11) | (2.36) | (2.45) | (2.18) | (2.12) | (2.36) | (2.45) |
| Classroom: Children's work displayed on the walls[a,c] | 1.33 | 1.87* | 0.44 | 1.69 | 1.17 | 1.75* | 0.26 | 1.49 |
| | (1.03) | (1.00) | (1.11) | (1.16) | (1.03) | (1.00) | (1.11) | (1.16) |
| Classroom: Date on the board's is today's date[a,c] | 1.02 | 0.81 | 1.27 | 0.96 | 0.92 | 0.68 | 1.21 | 0.85 |
| | (1.24) | (1.20) | (1.34) | (1.39) | (1.24) | (1.20) | (1.34) | (1.39) |
| Classroom: Instructional materials posted on the walls[a,c] | 1.18 | 1.13 | 1.52 | 0.88 | 1.19 | 1.15 | 1.49 | 0.91 |
| | (1.01) | (0.98) | (1.09) | (1.14) | (1.01) | (0.98) | (1.09) | (1.14) |
| Classroom: Teacher present in the classroom[a,c] | 1.33 | 1.52 | 1.12 | 1.36 | 1.43 | 1.61 | 1.18 | 1.53 |
| | (1.33) | (1.29) | (1.44) | (1.49) | (1.33) | (1.29) | (1.44) | (1.49) |
| School has a PTR above 90 | −13.25** | −9.10 | −16.08** | −14.72** | −13.23** | −8.95 | −15.75** | −15.01** |
| | (6.41) | (6.20) | (6.92) | (7.20) | (6.41) | (6.21) | (6.93) | (7.19) |
| Total enrollment (per 100 students) | −0.75 | −0.77 | −0.52 | −0.97 | −0.90 | −0.90 | −0.69 | −1.15* |
| | (0.62) | (0.60) | (0.67) | (0.70) | (0.62) | (0.60) | (0.67) | (0.70) |
| Number of classroom blocks in school | 1.52 | 1.76 | 1.00 | 1.80 | 1.48 | 1.72 | 1.01 | 1.74 |
| | (1.28) | (1.24) | (1.38) | (1.44) | (1.28) | (1.24) | (1.38) | (1.44) |
| Number of teacher housing units in school | 0.59 | 0.53 | 0.51 | 0.72 | 0.71 | 0.63 | 0.65 | 0.85 |
| | (1.01) | (0.98) | (1.09) | (1.14) | (1.01) | (0.98) | (1.09) | (1.13) |
| Students with 1+ years of pre-primary education[a,c] | 4.40*** | 3.29*** | 5.19*** | 4.72*** | 4.40*** | 3.29*** | 5.21*** | 4.67*** |
| | (0.89) | (0.86) | (0.96) | (1.00) | (0.89) | (0.86) | (0.96) | (1.00) |
| School lacks female in leadership position | −11.25** | −10.70** | −10.32** | −12.76** | −11.07** | −10.45** | −10.26** | −12.48** |
| | (4.58) | (4.43) | (4.94) | (5.14) | (4.57) | (4.43) | (4.94) | (5.13) |
| Class size in grade 1 is above 100 | 17.25*** | 15.03*** | 18.69*** | 18.01*** | 16.82*** | 14.70** | 18.09*** | 17.64*** |
| | (5.97) | (5.78) | (6.45) | (6.71) | (5.97) | (5.79) | (6.45) | (6.70) |
| *d. Students' characteristics (L1)* | | | | | | | | |
| Student above median age | | | | | −7.91*** | −11.03*** | −3.94 | −8.74*** |
| | | | | | (2.01) | (2.29) | (2.46) | (2.48) |
| Student is female | | | | | −18.87*** | −19.90*** | −24.54*** | −12.15*** |
| | | | | | (1.83) | (2.09) | (2.25) | (2.27) |
| Student is above median SES | | | | | 1.75 | 7.40*** | 0.63 | −2.74 |
| | | | | | (1.96) | (2.23) | (2.40) | (2.42) |

*continued*

TABLE 2A.3, *continued*

| CHARACTERISTIC | WITH CHARACTERISTICS ESTIMATED AT SCHOOL LEVEL | | | | WITH ADDITION OF INDIVIDUAL STUDENT CHARACTERISTICS | | | |
|---|---|---|---|---|---|---|---|---|
| | OVERALL | ENGLISH | MATH | CHICHEWA | OVERALL | ENGLISH | MATH | CHICHEWA |
| Number of times student has repeated any grade (grade 1–4) | | | | | −8.74*** | −7.75*** | −6.22*** | −12.23*** |
| | | | | | (1.03) | (1.17) | (1.26) | (1.27) |
| Student has at least one parent literate | | | | | 4.93** | 0.88 | 7.43*** | 6.48** |
| | | | | | (2.22) | (2.52) | (2.72) | (2.74) |
| Student speaks Chichewa at home | | | | | 4.87 | 4.39 | 7.15* | 3.07 |
| | | | | | (3.43) | (3.91) | (4.21) | (4.24) |
| Student receives help from parents on homework at home | | | | | −1.30 | −2.46 | 1.14 | −2.57 |
| | | | | | (2.01) | (2.29) | (2.47) | (2.48) |
| Student was absent on any day last week | | | | | −12.42*** | −11.48*** | −12.16*** | −13.61*** |
| | | | | | (2.04) | (2.33) | (2.51) | (2.53) |
| Raw Raven Test Score (0–6 scale) | | | | | 6.54*** | 5.98*** | 6.90*** | 6.75*** |
| | | | | | (0.69) | (0.78) | (0.84) | (0.85) |
| Student agrees that "You are interested in talking to new kids in school" describes them[a,c] | | | | | 9.65*** | 7.85*** | 12.27*** | 8.84*** |
| | | | | | (2.44) | (2.78) | (2.99) | (3.02) |
| Student agrees that "When you start your homework you tend to finish it" describes them[a,c] | | | | | 17.72*** | 11.34*** | 23.55*** | 18.32*** |
| | | | | | (3.79) | (4.31) | (4.65) | (4.68) |
| Student agrees that "Failing in a test frustrates you" describes them[a,c] | | | | | 9.77*** | 5.93** | 15.39*** | 7.99** |
| | | | | | (2.58) | (2.93) | (3.16) | (3.19) |
| Student agrees that "Teachers or parents often tell you that you are not performing to your potential" describes them | | | | | −9.51*** | −8.93*** | −7.39*** | −12.21*** |
| | | | | | (2.29) | (2.61) | (2.81) | (2.83) |
| Constant | 305.40*** | 322.52*** | 288.87*** | 302.60*** | 310.02*** | 328.46*** | 286.08*** | 312.05*** |
| | (81.09) | (78.50) | (87.63) | (91.12) | (81.10) | (78.69) | (87.72) | (91.03) |
| Division fixed effects | Yes | Yes | Yes | Yes | Yes | Yes | Yes | Yes |
| *Observations* | | | | | | | | |
| Schools (L2) | 482 | 482 | 482 | 482 | 482 | 482 | 482 | 482 |
| Students (L1) | 11,988 | 11,988 | 11,988 | 11,988 | 11,920 | 11,920 | 11,920 | 11,920 |
| *Null_Model_Variance* | | | | | | | | |
| Total variance | 13,484 | 15,876 | 18,877 | 19,169 | 13,484 | 15,876 | 18,877 | 19,169 |
| Schools (L2) | 3,411 | 2,908 | 3,769 | 3,968 | 3,411 | 2,908 | 3,769 | 3,968 |
| Students (L1) (residual) | 10,073 | 12,968 | 15,108 | 15,201 | 10,073 | 12,968 | 15,108 | 15,201 |
| *Model_Intraclass_Correlation_ICC* | | | | | | | | |
| ICC estimate | 0.25 | 0.18 | 0.20 | 0.21 | 0.25 | 0.18 | 0.20 | 0.21 |
| ICC standard error | 0.01 | 0.01 | 0.01 | 0.01 | 0.01 | 0.01 | 0.01 | 0.01 |

*continued*

TABLE 2A.3, continued

| CHARACTERISTIC | WITH CHARACTERISTICS ESTIMATED AT SCHOOL LEVEL | | | | WITH ADDITION OF INDIVIDUAL STUDENT CHARACTERISTICS | | | |
|---|---|---|---|---|---|---|---|---|
| | OVERALL | ENGLISH | MATH | CHICHEWA | OVERALL | ENGLISH | MATH | CHICHEWA |
| *Random_Intercepts_Model_Variance* | | | | | | | | |
| Total variance | 11,741 | 14,347 | 16,865 | 17,205 | 11,336 | 13,960 | 16,363 | 16,764 |
| Schools (L2) | 1,701 | 1,452 | 1,853 | 2,047 | 1,711 | 1,470 | 1,869 | 2,049 |
| Students (L1) (residual) | 10,040 | 12,895 | 15,012 | 15,158 | 9,625 | 12,490 | 14,494 | 14,715 |
| *Model_Intraclass_Correlation_ICC* | | | | | | | | |
| ICC estimate | 0.14 | 0.10 | 0.11 | 0.12 | 0.15 | 0.11 | 0.11 | 0.12 |
| ICC standard error | 0.01 | 0.01 | 0.01 | 0.01 | 0.01 | 0.01 | 0.01 | 0.01 |
| *Model_R_squared* | | | | | | | | |
| School level (L2) | 0.50 | 0.50 | 0.51 | 0.48 | 0.50 | 0.49 | 0.50 | 0.48 |
| Student level (L1) | 0.00 | 0.01 | 0.01 | 0.00 | 0.04 | 0.04 | 0.04 | 0.03 |

*Source:* Malawi Longitudinal School Survey internal (2016) data.
*Note:* Rural schools only; 27 schools with incomplete data are excluded. Coefficients from hierarchical linear modeling regressions estimated using random intercepts adjusted by student-level (L1) and school-level (L2) variables. Intercept represents the expected school average score when continuous predictors are set at mean value and dummy indicators at zero. School level columns are blank in Panel D because estimations were calculated only at student level. IQI = infrastructure quality index; PTR = pupil-teacher ratio; SES = socioeconomic status; SLM = student learning materials; TLM = teaching and learning materials.
a. School-level share.
b. School-level average.
c. Per 10 percentage points.
d. The IQI is a principal component analysis (PCA) index assigned to each school based on the use of open–air classrooms and the materials and condition of walls, roofs, floors, windows, and doors in classrooms.
e. The TLM index is a PCA index constructed at classroom level from binary items based on whether classroom has a blackboard, chalk, a chair or desk for the teacher, or a learning materials corner. Index is averaged at the school level.
f. The SLM index is a PCA index constructed from dichotomic items using the following thresholds: share of students with pen or pencil or notebook above the median; share of students with uniforms above the median; pupil–desk ratio of 3 to 1 or above; and pupil–textbook ratio of 4 to 1 or above.
*$p < .10$ **$p < .05$ ***$p < .01$

## NOTES

1. The MLSS collected a wide range of information on conditions in Malawi's schools, including the number and condition of buildings; the availability of basic amenities, such as electricity and water; accessibility and distance to nearby trading centers and amenities; and availability of handwashing and sanitation facilities. The MLSS also observed conditions inside more than 4,700 classrooms, noting the state of walls, floors, and roofs and the presence of key classroom facilities such as blackboards, chalk, and learning materials. For all these summary statistics, refer to annex 2A.
2. As elsewhere throughout this report, "typical" refers to the median. Unless otherwise stated, all specified statistics are for rural schools only.
3. Even in schools with an ostensible source of drinking water, the quality of water varies considerably, according to head teachers interviewed for the MLSS.
4. A similar pattern persists for uniforms, with 31 percent of grade 1 students having a uniform on average versus 53 percent in grade 5 and 61 percent in grade 8.
5. Of the grade 1 classrooms, 61.2 percent have zero textbooks observed—a condition that also applies to 56.9 percent of grade 2, 20.3 percent of grade 7, and 19.2 percent of grade 8 classrooms.
6. Seventeen percent of remote schools are close to a road of tarmac or gravel, versus 44 percent of schools close to a trading center. Twenty-seven percent of remote schools typically become inaccessible, versus only 8 percent of schools close to a trading center.
7. Eighty-eight percent of remote schools have no electricity access versus 65 percent of schools close to a trading center, and 47 percent lack handwashing facilities versus 43 percent of schools close to a trading center.

8. Remote schools have an average pupil-classroom ratio of 106 pupils to a classroom, versus 132 for schools close to a trading center. Remote schools are not significantly more likely than schools close to a trading center to have classes in the open air: 7 percent of class areas are open-air in both remote schools and in those close to a trading center.
9. Significantly fewer students in remote schools than in schools close to a trading center wear a uniform (43 percent versus 49 percent of students). However, there are no significant differences in availability of chairs or textbooks, and only a small variation in availability of notebooks and pencils.
10. At remote schools, 68 percent of classroom walls are in fine condition, versus 78 percent in schools close to the trading center; a similar pattern is observed for floors (40 percent versus 49 percent).
11. At remote schools, 85 percent of classrooms have chalk, versus 93 percent in schools close to the trading center; for a teachers' chair, the shares are 81 percent versus 92 percent; and for a learning materials corner, 20 percent versus 29 percent.
12. The typical school received MK 699,000 (US$950 at the time) in SIGs in 2015/16, equivalent to financing of only MK 878 (US$1.19) per student, and had a bank account balance when surveyed of just MK 16,000 (US$18) (refer to annex 2A, table 2A.2).
13. In 2014/15, remote schools received SIG transfers 21 days later than the average school, whereas schools close to a trading center received SIG transfers an average of 14 days earlier than the average school.
14. Among the schools close to a trading center, 31 percent of schools received visits from an inspector, whereas only 10 percent of remote schools received such visits. And 38.5 percent of schools close to a trading center were visited by a District Education Manager versus 12.5 percent of remote schools.
15. Estimates using longitudinal data demonstrate that students' learning increases by an average of approximately 50–55 points per year (Asim, Bashir, and Casley Gera, forthcoming). Across subjects, students in remote schools achieve composite scores an average 39 points lower than in schools close to a trading center (477 versus 518), equivalent to approximately nine months' learning.
16. A hierarchical linear modeling multilevel model including school, teacher, and student characteristics collapsed at the school level as well as individual student characteristics. For the full set of variables, see annex 2A, table 2A.3. Results are in line with seemingly unrelated regressions and ordinary least squares. For additional details, see appendix A.
17. Innate intelligence is measured using Raven's Progressive Matrices, a common measure. For details, refer to the technical appendix (https://openknowledge.worldbank.org/handle/10986/40948).
18. We define an SLM index based on the availability of desks, textbooks, pens and notebooks, and uniforms. For details, see annex 2A, table 2A.3, panel c.
19. For more information about how the Malawi Education Reform Program incorporates the findings of the MLSS, refer to chapter 6.

## REFERENCES

Asim, S., S. Bashir, and R. Casley Gera. Forthcoming. "Learning Loss as a Result of COVID-19: Dynamic Analysis from Malawi." Unpublished manuscript, World Bank, Washington, DC.

Asim, S., J. Chimombo, D. Chugunov, and R. Gera. 2019. "Moving Teachers to Malawi's Remote Communities: A Data-Driven Approach to Teacher Deployment." *International Journal of Educational Development* 65: 26–43.

Bashir, S., M. Lockheed, E. Ninan, and J. Tan. 2018. *Facing Forward: Schooling for Learning in Africa*. Washington, DC: World Bank.

MoE (Malawi, Ministry of Education). 2023. "2023 Malawi Education Statistics Report." Lilongwe, Malawi.

MoEST (Malawi, Ministry of Education, Science and Technology). 2014. "Education Statistics 2014." Lilongwe, Malawi.

# 3 Teachers
## LEARNING CONSTRAINTS FROM LARGE CLASS SIZES

**KEY POINTS**

The Malawi Longitudinal School Survey (MLSS) baseline data reveal that, although Malawi has an almost adequate number of teachers, they are extremely poorly utilized.[1] As chapter 2 showed, teachers are unevenly distributed between schools, with remote schools having much higher pupil-teacher ratios (PTRs). Further analysis in this chapter shows that, within schools, teachers are poorly distributed between grades.

Teachers also show high rates of absence and low levels of time spent teaching. When they do teach, teachers exhibit positive learning practices; however, faced with large class sizes, teachers often choose not to use teaching practices that are time-intensive on a per-student basis, like marking homework. However, new reforms and investments are beginning to tackle large class sizes.

**POOR DISTRIBUTION OF TEACHERS BETWEEN GRADES**

Teacher quality is perhaps the most important input for learning (Bold et al. 2017). Teachers also represent by far Malawi's largest investment in education, representing more than 70 percent of basic education spending (World Bank 2020). However, this investment is being poorly utilized.

The typical Malawian primary school has an almost adequate number of teachers, but they are poorly distributed between grades. The typical school has 11 teachers, of whom 3 are female.[2] The median school PTR is 65 to 1, just above the government's target of 60 to 1. However, poor distribution of teachers among grades causes severe shortages in lower grades and comparative overstaffing in upper grades.[3]

The typical school has 163 students in grade 1, 124 in grade 2, and only 47 in grade 8. Despite this large variation in enrollment, the typical school has fewer than two teachers in grades 1–2 and two or more teachers in grade 8.[4] PTRs in the typical school are almost four times higher in grade 1 than in grade 8 (figure 3.1). As a result, class sizes at a typical school (including both indoor and open-air

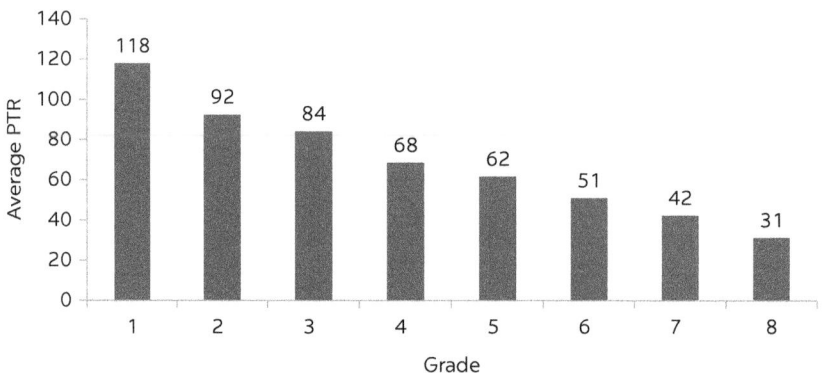

FIGURE 3.1
**Average PTR, by grade, 2016**

Source: Malawi Longitudinal School Survey baseline (2016) data.
Note: Data include both rural and urban schools. PTR = pupil-teacher ratio.

classes) are as high as 139 in grade 1, but they are just 59 in a typical grade 7. In addition to lacking teachers, lower-primary grades (grades 1–4) in the typical school also are open for fewer hours each day than upper-primary grades (grades 5–8).[5]

Our two case study schools illustrate this disproportionate distribution of teachers between grades. At Kamulindeni school, although 219 of the school's 353 students (62 percent) are enrolled in grades 1–4, only three out of its seven teachers teach these grades. The result is that, although the overall school PTR is 50 to 1, the lower-primary PTR is substantially higher (73 to 1). Similarly, at Chamkoko school, although 269 of 420 enrolled students (64 percent) are in lower-primary school, only two of five teachers teach in lower primary; and although the overall PTR is high (84 to 1), the lower-primary PTR is much higher (134 to 1).

In addition, female teachers are unlikely to be assigned to upper grades or to leadership positions. Fifty-five percent of the teachers who teach grade 1 regularly are female, but only 10 percent of grade 8 teachers are female. This distribution represents a severe lack of role models for female students in the upper grades, which may contribute to high dropout rates (Beaman et al. 2012). In remote schools, these effects combine with a general lack of female teachers to lead to severe shortages of female teachers in the upper grades (as discussed in chapter 2, box 2.1). In addition, female teachers are severely underrepresented in school leadership positions: although 49 percent of teachers at MLSS-sampled schools are female, only 8 percent of sampled schools have a female head teacher, and 46 percent have no female head teacher, deputy head teacher, or section head.

These weaknesses in allocation of teachers demonstrate a failure of the education system to provide clear and consistent guidance to head teachers on the correct utilization of staff. Although official policy is that teachers should be allocated equitably across grades, head teachers push teachers to upper grades to maximize student performance in the Primary School Leaving Certificate Examinations, the national examination conducted in grade 8 that governs progression to secondary school.

## TEACHER ABSENCE AND INADEQUATE TEACHING TIME

Malawi's teachers are often absent from school and, when in school, spend an inadequate amount of time in the classroom. Evidence from a wide range of Sub-Saharan countries shows that teacher practices are the key driver of educational attainment (Bold et al. 2017).[6] In many of the region's countries, teachers are frequently absent or not in class and, when *in* class, are often not teaching (Bashir et al. 2018). The MLSS confirms that Malawi is no exception to this problem. Thirteen percent of teachers at sampled schools were absent on the day of data collection. Teachers' own estimations suggest that the typical Malawian teacher spends just 2.4 hours per day, less than half the school day, teaching their own class.[7] Ten percent said they spent less than 30 minutes each day teaching.

The MLSS classroom observations were carried out during scheduled lesson time; however, in 50 percent of observed classrooms, the teacher was not present when the MLSS observer entered, and in 11 percent of lessons, the teacher never arrived and the lesson never took place.[8] Once lessons began, the teacher typically spent only about four-fifths of the allotted lesson time—31–33 minutes of the scheduled 40 minutes—actually engaged in teaching activities. In 10 percent of observed lessons, the teacher was engaged in actual teaching activities for half or less of the allotted lesson time.[9]

Delays in salary payments are frequent and a likely driver of low teacher effort. The large majority of teachers in the MLSS baseline (88 percent) had unpaid or delayed salary claims outstanding. Teachers in remote schools are more likely than those in schools close to trading centers to have experienced salary delays in the last year.[10] Furthermore, poor systems of supervision, as described in chapter 2, likely contribute to the persistence of low teaching time in remote schools.

## ADAPTATION OF TEACHING STRATEGIES FOR LARGE CLASS SIZES

In general, teachers have a barely adequate level of subject knowledge. The MLSS asked teachers to complete the same assessment exercise given to grade 4 students. The median teacher achieved a score of 96 percent in English and 93 percent in mathematics and Chichewa, showing satisfactory (though imperfect) knowledge of the concepts covered in lower-primary school curricula. However, a minority of teachers scored significantly below this level: the bottom 10 percent of performers scored less than 89 percent in English, 82 percent in mathematics, and 81 percent in Chichewa.

When present in the classroom, Malawi's primary school teachers exhibit a range of positive teaching practices.[11] These teachers, when teaching, are as likely as those in comparable countries to engage in positive behaviors associated with improved learning, such as correcting mistakes and giving positive reinforcement, and Malawian teachers are among the most likely to ask questions of students (figure 3.2).[12]

FIGURE 3.2

**Shares of primary school teachers using selected practices, Malawi and other Sub-Saharan African countries, 2016**

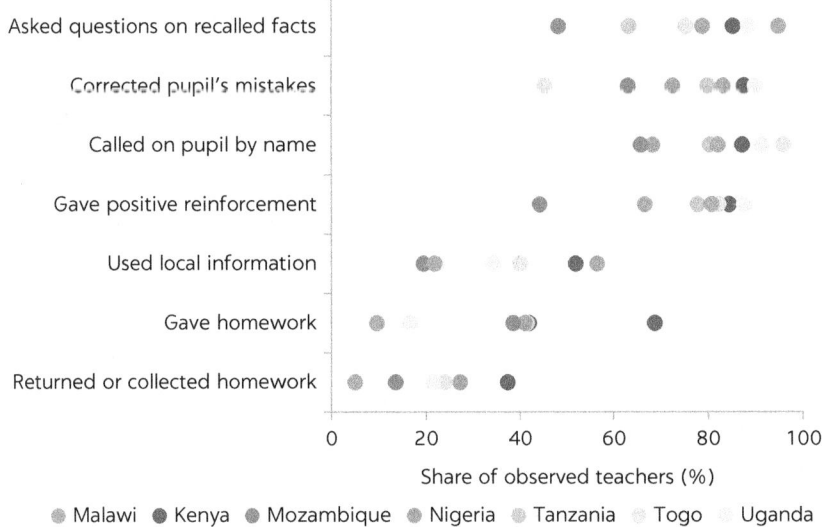

Source: Malawi Longitudinal School Survey baseline (2016) data; World Bank Service Delivery Indicators survey data.

However, Malawian teachers are less likely than those in comparable countries to use teaching aids and to assign or mark homework. Only about one-quarter of teachers in rural schools (24 percent) use teaching aids such as posters and models to support learning; a similar share (23 percent) use local information and resources from the community to make learning relevant to students; and only 60 percent of teachers refrained from scolding students for mistakes (refer to annex 3A, table 3A.2).

Only 9 percent of teachers in observed lessons set homework for students. More concerning still, only 5 percent collected or reviewed homework previously assigned to students, suggesting that thousands of teachers may be routinely giving homework that is never marked. In the MLSS student interviews, only 50 percent of students said that their teachers were available after class to provide them with additional help.

In our case study schools, teachers used teaching aids in two out of four classes observed by MLSS enumerators but did not use local information and resources in any of the observed classes, and teachers scolded students at least once in three out of the four classes. The teacher did not set, collect, or mark homework in any of four classes observed by MLSS observers.

Teaching practices are limited by large class sizes. The findings suggest that teachers, although performing adequately when addressing their entire classes, avoid tasks that require completion on a per-student basis, such as marking homework or providing support after class. This practice likely reflects the large class sizes teachers often face, which limit the ability of teachers to engage meaningfully with all pupils. Box 3.1 presents more information on large class sizes from the teachers' perspectives.

### BOX 3.1

### Teachers' perspectives on large class sizes

To capture the experience of teaching large classes in Malawi's primary schools, we interviewed six lower-primary teachers from two schools: Thunga and Mankhamba, both in the Thunga zone in Thyolo district. The interviewed teachers' class sizes ranged from 102 to 174 at Mankhamba and from 78 to 125 at Thunga.

All six teachers reported that teaching large class sizes is challenging and believe that their teaching behaviors would be different if their class sizes were smaller. In particular, all of the teachers agreed that they would give and mark homework more frequently if their class sizes were smaller. As one teacher said, "The issue is time. The bigger the class, the more time you need for marking."

Five out of the six teachers also felt that their classroom management would improve with smaller class sizes. "It's easy for learners to fight in a large class, whereas if learners are few, you can easily notice who is misbehaving and so it becomes easier to control them," said one. Individual teachers also named additional challenges with large class sizes, including the difficulties of knowing each student well enough to understand and address their weaknesses and of monitoring and intervening on student absenteeism.

Only two out of the six said that they received training in strategies for teaching large class sizes, though all six reported using group work and student leaders to maximize learning in their large classes. However, as one teacher explained, "Even the groups require teacher supervision, and it is not easy to walk around the classroom to make sure that all learners are on task and offer help in the groups when it is needed."

Most teachers said that they would be more satisfied with their jobs if their class sizes were smaller. As one teacher explained, "Teaching a large class is overwhelming because when you teach the learners, you expect that you will produce more achievers than failures, but this is harder in a large class than a small class." This comment may suggest that large class sizes are a driver of low teacher motivation and, as a result, effort.

Finally, all of the teachers felt that a lack of adequate teaching and learning materials exacerbates the problem of large class sizes, making it even more challenging to help learners understand concepts and stay engaged.

*Note:* The teacher interviews were conducted by Linda Matumbi of the World Bank.

## WHAT MATTERS FOR LEARNING?

We conducted regression analysis to identify the teacher characteristics (as shown in chapter 2, annex 2A, table 2A.3, panel b) and teaching practices (shown in annex 3A, table 3A.3) most commonly associated with higher learning outcomes.[13] Table 3.1 summarizes the key findings.

### Teacher characteristics

**Junior teachers produce lower learning outcomes.** An increase of ten percentage points in the share of teachers at a school who are PT4 (the most junior level for qualified teachers in Malawi) or are an unqualified teaching assistant is associated with a 3.6 point decline in student knowledge scores. This finding suggests that the government's current approach to addressing PTR disparities, which depends on allocating newly deployed teachers to remote schools, is unlikely to produce equitable learning outcomes without complementary action to maintain more senior teachers in remote schools.

TABLE 3.1 **Correlation of achievement gaps with teacher characteristics and practices, 2016**

| TEACHER CHARACTERISTIC (SCHOOL LEVEL) | ADJUSTED STUDENT KNOWLEDGE SCORE | |
| --- | --- | --- |
| | BOTTOM QUINTILE OF SCHOOLS | TOP QUINTILE OF SCHOOLS |
| *a. Correlation with teacher characteristics*[a] | | |
| Share of junior teachers* | **498** | **508** |
| Share of teachers living in same district as school* | **496** | **509** |
| Number of salary delays in last 12 months* | **497** | **510** |
| Average teacher age | 504 | 502 |
| Average years of teacher tenure | 501 | 505 |
| Average mathematics content knowledge | 504 | 502 |
| | ADJUSTED STUDENT KNOWLEDGE SCORE | |
| TEACHING PRACTICE | NO | YES |
| *b. Correlation with teaching practices*[b] | | |
| Teacher uses teaching aids* | **496** | **521** |
| Students ask questions of teacher about the lesson* | **497** | **520** |
| Teacher politely corrects mistakes | 495 | 503 |
| Children's work displayed on walls | 503 | 499 |
| Instructional materials posted on walls | 499 | 505 |

*Source:* Calculations from Malawi Longitudinal School Survey baseline (2016) data.
*Note:* In panel a, "Top" and "bottom" quintiles are in terms of the indicated characteristic. For panel b, "top" and "bottom" quintiles refer to the top and bottom 20 percent of schools in terms of whether each practice was used in the observed lessons. **Bold** and * indicate that the estimated adjusted score gap, statistically, is significantly different from zero. ($p = .05$)
a. Panel shows the adjusted scores associated with different shares of teachers with particular characteristics in a school, controlling for a wide range of school, teacher, and student characteristics.
b. Panel shows the adjusted scores associated with different teachers' practices included in the regression model, which also included the average knowledge score of students across mathematics and English in the observed classrooms.

**Teacher knowledge is not predictive of student learning.** The average performance of a school's teachers on the MLSS English and mathematics assessments is not significantly associated with student learning outcomes at the school in the same assessments. This finding reflects the relatively low variation in knowledge levels among sampled teachers, as described earlier.

**Salary delays are associated with lower learning outcomes.** Students in schools with a higher frequency of delayed salary payments to teachers achieve lower learning outcomes. For every additional delay to monthly salaries (averaged across all sampled teachers in a school), students achieve scores that are six points lower overall. This achievement gap persists when controlling for school remoteness. This finding suggests that efforts to address salary delays, by improving teacher motivation and effort, can raise learning outcomes.[14]

### Teaching practices

**Teaching aids boost learning.** Efforts by teachers to complement textbooks and instruction with additional materials have large benefits for learning. Students whose teachers use teaching aids such as posters or models achieve learning scores averaging 26 points higher than those whose teachers do not, equivalent to about six months' additional learning. However, significant impacts were not observed from the display of instructional materials, such as maps and charts, on classroom walls.

**Teachers who encourage students to ask questions also achieve higher learning outcomes.** Classes in which students ask questions of the teacher achieve average learning scores 23 points higher than those where students do not (regardless of whether the teacher asks questions of students).

## CONCLUSIONS: INEQUITIES IN SCHOOLS' TEACHER DISTRIBUTION, MANAGEMENT, AND PERFORMANCE

The MLSS findings reveal significant problems of teacher distribution and utilization in Malawi's primary schools:

- Teachers, particularly male teachers, are overconcentrated in upper grades despite extremely large class sizes in lower grades.
- Malawian teachers are frequently not found in the classroom during their allotted teaching time and, when in the classroom, are not consistently found teaching.
- When they do teach, Malawian teachers are as likely as those in similar countries to employ a range of positive teaching practices.
- However, teachers are less likely to assign or mark homework and to assist students after class. This finding suggests that large class sizes are reducing the capacity or willingness of teachers to conduct more time-intensive teaching activities.

Informed by the insights from the MLSS, new reforms have begun to tackle large class sizes and other barriers to effective teaching. Under the Malawi Education Reform Program, schools with severe overcrowding will receive grant financing for construction of classrooms and hiring of auxiliary teachers, substantially reducing the share of schools with extremely large class sizes in the lower-primary grades. In addition, schools have been given clearer policy guidance on the allocation of teachers between grades, and School Leadership Program training for head teachers, deputy head teachers, and Primary Education Advisers supports school leaders to better allocate, supervise, and manage teachers (as discussed in box I.1 in the introduction to this report).

## ANNEX 3A STATISTICAL AND REGRESSION TABLES

TABLE 3A.1 **Summary statistics on teacher characteristics**

| CHARACTERISTIC | TEACHERS IN ALL RURAL SCHOOLS (N = 4,417) | | | | | TEACHERS IN REMOTE SCHOOLS (n = 832) | | TEACHERS IN SCHOOLS CLOSE TO TC (n = 840) | |
|---|---|---|---|---|---|---|---|---|---|
| | MEAN | SD | P10 | P50 | P90 | MEAN | SD | MEAN | SD |
| Teacher is female (%) | 46 | 50 | 0.00 | 0.00 | 100 | 30 | 46 | 62 | 49 |
| Age of teacher (years) | 34.22 | 9.83 | 23.00 | 31.00 | 48.00 | 34.5 | 9.9 | 35.8 | 10.0 |
| Teacher is PT4[a] (%) | 76 | 43 | 0.00 | 100 | 100 | 77 | 42 | 70 | 46 |
| Teacher training level is IPTE or ODL (%) | 53 | 50 | 0.00 | 100 | 100 | 51 | 50 | 48 | 50 |
| Teacher tenure at school (years) | 4.14 | 4.97 | 0.00 | 3.00 | 11.00 | 4.3 | 5.4 | 4.8 | 5.7 |
| Teacher from same district as school (%) | 58 | 49 | 0.00 | 100 | 100 | 66 | 47 | 51 | 50 |

*continued*

TABLE 3A.1, continued

| CHARACTERISTIC | TEACHERS IN ALL RURAL SCHOOLS (N = 4,417) | | | | | TEACHERS IN REMOTE SCHOOLS (n = 832) | | TEACHERS IN SCHOOLS CLOSE TO TC (n = 840) | |
|---|---|---|---|---|---|---|---|---|---|
| | MEAN | SD | P10 | P50 | P90 | MEAN | SD | MEAN | SD |
| Teacher commuting time to school (minutes) | 20.45 | 17.34 | 11.25 | 11.25 | 37.50 | 17.7 | 15.1 | 18.9 | 15.4 |
| Number of salary delays in the last 12 months | 2.73 | 2.62 | 0.00 | 2.00 | 6.00 | 2.8 | 2.8 | 2.6 | 2.5 |
| Teacher English content knowledge (percentage points) | 94.16 | 8.49 | 88.46 | 96.15 | 100.00 | 94.5 | 6.1 | 94.4 | 8.8 |
| Teacher mathematics content knowledge (percentage points) | 89.23 | 10.10 | 82.14 | 92.86 | 96.43 | 89.9 | 8.0 | 88.8 | 11.7 |
| Teacher's performance is assessed (%) | 74 | 44 | 0.00 | 100 | 100 | 73 | 44 | 75 | 43 |
| Teacher's performance is encouraged (%) | 44 | 50 | 0.00 | 0.00 | 100 | 46 | 50 | 46 | 50 |
| Teacher is satisfied with the job (%) | 80 | 40 | 0.00 | 100 | 100 | 82 | 38 | 81 | 40 |

Source: Malawi Longitudinal School Survey baseline (2016) data.
Note: See table 1A.1 for details of included schools and chapter 2 for definitions of "remote" and "close to TC" schools. IPTE = Initial Primary Teacher Education; ODL = Open Distance Learning; P10 = 10th percentile; P50 = 50th percentile; P90 = 90th percentile; SD = standard deviation.
a. "PT4" denotes teachers with the lowest teaching grade, as well as student teachers and unqualified teacher assistants.

### TABLE 3A.2 Summary statistics of teacher practices in lessons observed

| CHARACTERISTICS OF LESSONS OBSERVED (%) | LESSONS OBSERVED IN ALL RURAL SCHOOLS (N = 829) | | | | | LESSONS IN REMOTE SCHOOLS (n = 177) | | LESSONS IN SCHOOLS CLOSE TO TC (n = 146) | |
|---|---|---|---|---|---|---|---|---|---|
| | MEAN | SD | P10 | P50 | P90 | MEAN | SD | MEAN | SD |
| Teacher present and teaching | 34 | 47 | 0.00 | 0.00 | 100 | 39 | 49 | 41 | 49 |
| Teacher present but not teaching | 10 | 30 | 0.00 | 0.00 | 0.00 | 5 | 23 | 14 | 35 |
| Teacher used textbook | 92 | 27 | 100 | 100 | 100 | 93 | 26 | 89 | 31 |
| Teacher used local information to make learning relevant | 23 | 42 | 0.00 | 0.00 | 100 | 23 | 42 | 20 | 40 |
| Teacher used any teaching aids | 24 | 43 | 0.00 | 0.00 | 100 | 22 | 0.41 | 31 | 46 |
| Teacher got student engagement and offered individual feedback | 78 | 41 | 0.00 | 100 | 100 | 72 | 45 | 83 | 38 |
| Teacher was smiling, laughing, or joking with pupils | 62 | 49 | 0.00 | 100 | 100 | 63 | 48 | 53 | 50 |
| Teacher asked questions to monitor students' understanding | 95 | 23 | 100 | 100 | 100 | 94 | 25 | 92 | 27 |
| Students asked questions of teacher regarding the lesson | 21 | 41 | 0.00 | 0.00 | 100 | 17 | 38 | 28 | 45 |
| Teacher gave positive feedback | 80 | 40 | 0.00 | 100 | 100 | 79 | 41 | 80 | 40 |
| Teacher politely corrected mistakes | 83 | 38 | 0.00 | 100 | 100 | 81 | 39 | 82 | 39 |
| Teacher never scolded students for mistakes | 60 | 49 | 0.00 | 100 | 100 | 71 | 46 | 57 | 50 |
| Teacher assigned homework | 09 | 29 | 0.00 | 0.00 | 0.00 | 11 | 31 | 8 | 27 |
| Teacher reviewed or collected homework | 5 | 22 | 0.00 | 0.00 | 0.00 | 3 | 17 | 5 | 23 |
| Date on the board was that day's date | 91 | 29 | 100 | 100 | 100 | 89 | 31 | 88 | 33 |
| Children's work displayed on the walls | 30 | 46 | 0.00 | 0.00 | 100 | 28 | 45 | 37 | 48 |
| Instructional materials posted on the walls | 48 | 50 | 0.00 | 0.00 | 100 | 50 | 50 | 61 | 49 |

Source: Malawi Longitudinal School Survey internal baseline (2016) data.
Note: Includes rural schools with complete data (456 schools, of which 98 were remote and 80 were close to TC). See chapter 2 for definitions of "remote" and "close to TC" schools. P10 = 10th percentile; P50 = 50th percentile; P90 = 90th percentile; SD = standard deviation.

TABLE 3A.3  Regression analysis of impact of teacher practices and characteristics on student knowledge scores, 2016

| PRACTICE OR CHARACTERISTIC | MATHEMATICS KNOWLEDGE SCORE | | | | ENGLISH KNOWLEDGE SCORE | | | | AVERAGE KNOWLEDGE SCORE ACROSS MATHEMATICS AND ENGLISH | | | |
|---|---|---|---|---|---|---|---|---|---|---|---|---|
| | BIVARIATE | MODEL 1 | MODEL 2 | MODEL 3 | BIVARIATE | MODEL 1 | MODEL 2 | MODEL 3 | BIVARIATE | MODEL 1 | MODEL 2 | MODEL 3 |
| *Practices of teachers in observed classrooms* | | | | | | | | | | | | |
| Teacher used any teaching aids | 29.12*** | 17.09** | 16.30** | 18.45*** | 12.06* | 5.35 | 6.83 | 12.86** | 31.75*** | 19.18** | 19.42*** | 25.84*** |
| | (7.27) | (7.24) | (6.68) | (6.17) | (7.31) | (7.19) | (6.55) | (6.20) | (8.14) | (8.06) | (7.32) | (6.78) |
| Students asked questions of teacher regarding the lesson | 15.07* | 5.67 | 18.63** | 23.51*** | 10.61 | 2.29 | 5.98 | 7.85 | 17.33** | 6.12 | 17.49** | 23.86*** |
| | (7.83) | (7.83) | (7.69) | (7.07) | (7.21) | (7.22) | (6.85) | (6.53) | (8.54) | (8.48) | (8.26) | (7.73) |
| Teacher politely gave feedback to correct mistake | 4.37 | −3.53 | −5.99 | −1.70 | 19.34** | 14.56* | 8.17 | 11.80 | 17.12* | 6.55 | 2.78 | 8.57 |
| | (8.07) | (7.74) | (7.36) | (6.75) | (8.29) | (8.20) | (7.62) | (7.24) | (9.59) | (9.28) | (8.63) | (8.04) |
| Teacher never scolded students on mistakes | −19.08*** | −15.26** | −9.37 | −6.15 | −14.36** | −4.61 | −4.03 | 2.65 | −24.93*** | −14.73** | −10.58 | −1.90 |
| | (6.60) | (6.48) | (6.36) | (5.87) | (5.92) | (6.21) | (5.87) | (5.62) | (7.00) | (7.11) | (6.86) | (6.48) |
| Children's work displayed on the walls | 24.17*** | 4.22 | −1.66 | −0.87 | 22.17*** | 1.06 | −7.70 | −6.31 | 24.04*** | 2.08 | −4.95 | −3.59 |
| | (6.96) | (8.23) | (8.47) | (7.74) | (6.36) | (7.68) | (7.85) | (7.43) | (6.36) | (7.58) | (7.65) | (7.07) |
| Instructional materials posted on the walls | 27.66*** | 22.09*** | 8.95 | 5.81 | 27.72*** | 24.52*** | 10.21 | 6.75 | 28.51*** | 23.56*** | 9.47 | 5.65 |
| | (6.31) | (7.51) | (8.34) | (7.69) | (5.78) | (7.01) | (7.67) | (7.28) | (5.69) | (6.86) | (7.51) | (6.96) |
| *Characteristics of teachers in observed classrooms* | | | | | | | | | | | | |
| Female teacher | 13.63** | 6.54 | −1.42 | 4.47 | 15.21** | 6.26 | −0.68 | −0.95 | 17.21*** | 9.31 | −0.18 | 1.24 |
| | (6.75) | (6.63) | (6.74) | (6.35) | (6.15) | (6.12) | (5.99) | (5.86) | (6.31) | (6.17) | (6.21) | (5.94) |
| Age of teacher (per 10 years) | −7.85** | 1.98 | −0.70 | 1.34 | −6.67** | 5.58 | 2.73 | 3.46 | −8.46*** | 4.45 | 0.54 | 2.25 |
| | (3.34) | (4.41) | (4.28) | (3.94) | (3.12) | (3.93) | (3.73) | (3.59) | (3.19) | (4.18) | (4.00) | (3.71) |
| Respondent is head teacher or deputy head teacher | −16.38* | −5.47 | 9.26 | 14.15 | −30.79*** | −26.81*** | −2.90 | −1.60 | −25.14*** | −17.46* | 3.99 | 6.81 |
| | (8.89) | (10.54) | (10.85) | (10.18) | (8.72) | (10.02) | (10.08) | (9.52) | (8.60) | (9.91) | (10.01) | (9.37) |
| Teacher number of children of primary age | −7.53*** | −5.50* | −2.85 | −2.16 | −7.28*** | −5.57** | −3.59 | −3.06 | −8.82*** | −6.80** | −3.75 | −3.35 |
| | (2.64) | (3.15) | (3.02) | (2.74) | (2.22) | (2.58) | (2.44) | (2.29) | (2.38) | (2.90) | (2.73) | (2.50) |
| Teacher lives in housing provided by school | −13.02* | −15.37** | −9.17 | −11.86* | −13.91** | −12.04* | −7.97 | −11.05* | −18.18*** | −16.06*** | −13.11* | −16.79*** |
| | (6.86) | (6.66) | (7.65) | (7.00) | (6.30) | (6.17) | (6.86) | (6.49) | (6.41) | (6.21) | (7.07) | (6.50) |

*continued*

48 | WHAT MATTERS FOR LEARNING IN MALAWI?

TABLE 3A.3, continued

| PRACTICE OR CHARACTERISTIC | MATHEMATICS KNOWLEDGE SCORE | | | | ENGLISH KNOWLEDGE SCORE | | | | AVERAGE KNOWLEDGE SCORE ACROSS MATHEMATICS AND ENGLISH | | | |
|---|---|---|---|---|---|---|---|---|---|---|---|---|
| | BIVARIATE | MODEL 1 | MODEL 2 | MODEL 3 | BIVARIATE | MODEL 1 | MODEL 2 | MODEL 3 | BIVARIATE | MODEL 1 | MODEL 2 | MODEL 3 |
| Teacher receives rural allowance | −14.44** | −9.09 | −19.48** | −19.85** | −13.67** | −5.37 | −7.51 | −3.50 | −14.69** | −6.37 | −13.59* | −10.97 |
| | (6.52) | (7.09) | (8.36) | (7.71) | (6.00) | (6.41) | (7.55) | (7.13) | (6.16) | (6.55) | (7.79) | (7.20) |
| Number of salary delays in the last 12 months | −3.56*** | −2.11** | 1.32 | 0.85 | −1.99** | −2.03** | 0.03 | 0.44 | −3.22*** | −2.18** | 0.26 | 0.45 |
| | (1.06) | (1.04) | (1.21) | (1.10) | (0.98) | (0.99) | (1.15) | (1.09) | (1.00) | (0.97) | (1.13) | (1.04) |
| Teacher was absent from school last month without first obtaining permission | −14.94* | −11.05 | −0.97 | −6.21 | −16.69** | −8.58 | −2.06 | −4.39 | −20.11*** | −14.85** | −3.27 | −9.13 |
| | (8.61) | (8.36) | (8.73) | (8.15) | (7.71) | (7.63) | (7.82) | (7.42) | (7.75) | (7.55) | (7.84) | (7.36) |
| Time spent on marking homework (log per 10 minutes change) | −23.21*** | −17.53*** | −14.68** | −11.61** | −18.80*** | −14.98*** | −11.05** | −7.79 | −24.10*** | −17.25*** | −16.19*** | −13.28*** |
| | (5.93) | (5.84) | (6.41) | (5.85) | (5.23) | (5.25) | (5.42) | (5.17) | (5.35) | (5.23) | (5.60) | (5.15) |
| Constant | | 536.62*** | 557.18*** | 281.08*** | | 500.26*** | 483.12*** | 158.54** | | 520.07*** | 509.64*** | 176.45** |
| | | (17.83) | (64.69) | (90.29) | | (16.25) | (55.68) | (76.48) | | (17.53) | (55.48) | (73.47) |
| Characteristics of teachers in observed classrooms[a] | | No | Yes | Yes | | No | Yes | Yes | | No | Yes | Yes |
| Characteristics of teachers in schools[b] | | No | Yes | Yes | | No | Yes | Yes | | No | Yes | Yes |
| Characteristics of schools | | No | Yes | Yes | | No | Yes | Yes | | No | Yes | Yes |
| Characteristics of students in schools[b] | | No | No | Yes | | No | No | Yes | | No | No | Yes |
| Characteristics of students in observed classrooms[c] | | No | Yes | Yes | | No | Yes | Yes | | No | Yes | Yes |
| Division fixed effects | | No | Yes | Yes | | No | Yes | Yes | | No | Yes | Yes |

*continued*

TABLE 3A.3, continued

| PRACTICE OR CHARACTERISTIC | MATHEMATICS KNOWLEDGE SCORE | | | | ENGLISH KNOWLEDGE SCORE | | | | AVERAGE KNOWLEDGE SCORE ACROSS MATHEMATICS AND ENGLISH | | | |
|---|---|---|---|---|---|---|---|---|---|---|---|---|
| | BIVARIATE | MODEL 1 | MODEL 2 | MODEL 3 | BIVARIATE | MODEL 1 | MODEL 2 | MODEL 3 | BIVARIATE | MODEL 1 | MODEL 2 | MODEL 3 |
| *Observations* | | | | | | | | | | | | |
| Classrooms (L2) | | 387 | 378 | 378 | | 383 | 375 | 375 | | 428 | 418 | 418 |
| Students (L1) | | 9,634 | 9,410 | 9,352 | | 9,530 | 9,330 | 9,274 | | 10,649 | 10,400 | 10,341 |
| *Random intercepts model variance* | | | | | | | | | | | | |
| Total variance | | 17,966 | 17,187 | 16,190 | | 15,318 | 14,606 | 13,875 | | 13,113 | 12,392 | 11,567 |
| Classroom level (L2) | | 2,885 | 2,096 | 1,597 | | 2,413 | 1,665 | 1,369 | | 2,570 | 1,814 | 1,442 |
| Student level (L1) (residual) | | 15,081 | 15,091 | 14,593 | | 12,905 | 12,941 | 12,505 | | 10,543 | 10,578 | 10,125 |
| *Model ICC* | | | | | | | | | | | | |
| ICC estimate | | 0.16 | 0.12 | 0.10 | | 0.16 | 0.11 | 0.10 | | 0.20 | 0.15 | 0.12 |
| ICC standard error | | 0.01 | 0.01 | 0.01 | | 0.01 | 0.01 | 0.01 | | 0.01 | 0.01 | 0.01 |
| *Model R squared* | | | | | | | | | | | | |
| Classroom level (L2) | | 0.20 | 0.42 | 0.56 | | 0.20 | 0.45 | 0.54 | | 0.21 | 0.44 | 0.56 |
| Student level (L1) | | 0.00 | 0.00 | 0.03 | | 0.00 | 0.00 | 0.03 | | 0.00 | 0.00 | 0.04 |

Source: World Bank calculations from Malawi Longitudinal School Survey baseline (2016) data.
Note: Includes rural schools with complete data (456 schools). Coefficients in this table correspond to random intercept hierarchical linear models of students (L1) nested within observed classrooms (L2). Model 1 adjusts by characteristics of the observed classrooms such as teacher practices and characteristics of the teacher teaching the subject. Model 2 adjusts by school and teacher characteristics. Model 3 is a full model that includes adjustments by characteristics of the students in the observed classrooms and characteristics aggregated to the school level. HSS = hardship support scheme; ICC = intraclass correlation coefficient.
a. Averages or shares calculated at school level (L2) for all teachers in observed classrooms.
b. Averages or shares calculated at school level (L2).
c. At student level (L1).
*$p < .10$ **$p < .05$ ***$p < .01$

## NOTES

1. The MLSS collected school-level data on staffing (including the number, seniority, and grade and subject allocations of teachers); conducted detailed interviews with more than 4,000 teachers about their personal and professional backgrounds, work experiences, work practices, and attitudes; and assessed their knowledge of curricula using the same specially designed learning assessment tools completed by students. In addition, observations were carried out of more than 1,000 grade 4 English and mathematics lessons, enabling the recording of teaching practices, use of teaching time, and interactions with students. For more details about the MLSS and its methodology, refer to the introduction's box I.2 and to appendix A.
2. As elsewhere throughout this report, "typical" refers to the median. Unless otherwise stated, all specified statistics are for rural schools only.
3. Malawi's primary school system has eight grades, although about one-quarter of schools—mostly in remote areas—do not offer the full range. Whereas district-level officials allocate teachers to *schools*, head teachers decide on the allocations of those teachers to particular *grades*. Most teachers primarily or exclusively teach one class, although cross-grade subject-specialist teachers do unofficially exist in larger schools.
4. Grade 1 averages 1.84 teachers, and grade 2, 1.79 teachers. Sixty-eight percent of schools employ more than one teacher in grade 8 despite having PTRs exceeding 80 to 1 in grades 1–2.
5. The median school is open for 6.2 hours per day for upper-primary classes and only 4.8 hours per day for lower-primary classes. This difference reflects Malawi's official standards, which require significantly less teaching time for the lower grades.
6. In addition to the interviews with more than 4,900 teachers and observations of more than 2,000 classrooms, the MLSS included full lesson observations for about 1,000 English and mathematics lessons—the most detailed picture of teaching practices in Malawi's schools ever recorded. For summary statistics on teaching practices observed in classrooms, see annex 3A, table 3A.2.
7. An additional 1.4 hours are spent preparing lessons, 0.85 hour marking homework, 0.85 hour on administrative duties, and 0.73 hour helping other teachers.
8. Observation began at the lesson's scheduled start time. If the teacher had not arrived after 20 minutes, the teacher was considered absent and the observation ceased. In a small number of cases, the teacher did arrive but no teaching took place.
9. In the 10 percent of observed lessons with the lowest observed teaching time, the teacher engaged in mathematics teaching activities for 21 minutes or less and in English teaching activities for 22 minutes or less. In general, across different estimations and subsets of schools, we observe no significant differences in teaching time between mathematics and English.
10. In remote schools, 80 percent of teachers reported at least one delay versus 75 percent of teachers in schools close to trading centers. "Remote schools" are the 20 percent of MLSS schools farthest from the nearest trading center (at least 9 kilometers away). "Schools close to a trading center" are the 20 percent of schools that are less than 2.9 kilometers away from the nearest trading center. The MLSS analysis uses the National Statistical Office of Malawi's official classification of more than 200 locations as trading centers. We measure the distance from a school to the nearest trading center using a geographic database developed from administrative data (Asim et al. 2019).
11. The MLSS lesson observation tool was adapted from that employed by the Service Delivery Indicators Survey, enabling robust comparison with data from countries where that survey was conducted.
12. To achieve comparability, the MLSS data collection tool, in line with similar tools used in international surveys, asked whether a teacher ever exhibited a particular behavior: for example, if a teacher ever gave positive reinforcement to a child during the observed lesson. Therefore, the observations do not fully capture the frequency with which teachers exhibited these behaviors.
13. We control for teacher personal characteristics including age, gender, and content knowledge; student personal characteristics; and school characteristics such as infrastructure and student population.

14. A direct measure of teacher satisfaction—whereby teachers were asked, "Are you satisfied with your job?"—was not significantly predictive of learning outcomes. This measure had low variation, with 80 percent of teachers answering "yes," which suggests some survey bias.

## REFERENCES

Asim, S., J. Chimombo, D. Chugunov, and R. Gera. 2019. "Moving Teachers to Malawi's Remote Communities: A Data-Driven Approach to Teacher Deployment." *International Journal of Educational Development* 65: 26–43.

Bashir, S., M. Lockheed, E. Ninan, and J. Tan. 2018. *Facing Forward: Schooling for Learning in Africa*. Washington, DC: World Bank

Beaman, L., E. Duflo, R. Pande, and P. Topalova. 2012. "Female Leadership Raises Aspirations and Educational Attainment for Girls: A Policy Experiment in India." *Science* 335 (6068): 582–86.

Bold, T., D. Filmer, G. Martin, E. Molina, C. Rockmore, B. Stacy, J. Svensson, and W. Wane. 2017. "What Do Teachers Know and Do? Does It Matter? Evidence from Primary Schools in Africa." Policy Research Working Paper 7956, World Bank, Washington, DC.

World Bank. 2020. "Malawi Public Expenditure Review 2020: Strengthening Expenditure for Human Capital." Programmatic Public Expenditure Review, World Bank, Washington, DC.

# 4 Students
## THE IMPORTANCE OF HOME BACKGROUND AND SUPPORT

**KEY POINTS**

The Malawi Longitudinal School Survey (MLSS) baseline data provide the clearest picture ever collected of Malawi's students, focusing on their backgrounds, experiences, and attitudes.[1] The typical Malawian class contains students of a wide range of ages and backgrounds, creating challenges for teaching and learning. Differences in student populations contribute substantially to variation in learning outcomes between schools. In particular, schools with high proportions of students with literate parents, majority-language speakers, and students with a positive mindset achieve higher average learning scores.

This chapter discusses differences in *student populations* between schools and their impact on learning. Chapter 5 discusses differences between *individual students* within schools and their impact on learning, with an emphasis on gender.

## DIVERSITY OF MALAWI'S STUDENT POPULATION

### Socioeconomic status

The typical Malawian student is from a home without many basic facilities.[2] The typical student's family lacks beds, electricity, piped water, stove, and a television; however, it does have a radio, mobile phone, toilet, and bicycle.[3] Their household has chickens but not more expensive animals such as goats or cows. The typical student has a manageable 23-minute walk to attend school each day as a result of Malawi's dense distribution of schools (a median distance of 2.3 kilometers).

However, the socioeconomic backgrounds of students vary widely, and the differences between the wealthiest 10 percent and the poorest are stark. The wealthiest 10 percent of students come from homes with electricity, piped water, a television, a bed, goats, pigs, and cattle.[4] The poorest 10 percent have no basic assets at home, except a toilet in some cases. In addition, a minority of students (6 percent) travel for more than one hour to reach school each day.

### Parental presence, parental literacy, and language spoken at home

Only 71 percent of students live with both of their parents, and 11 percent live with neither. A large proportion of parents are not literate: only 68 percent of students have two parents at home who can read or write; 19 percent have only one literate parent.[5]

The typical student speaks Chichewa—the majority language and most common language of lower-primary instruction—at home, but 31 percent speak other languages.[6] Overall, fewer than half of Malawi's students come from families with two literate parents who speak the majority language.

Differences in student language background are common within a single class: in more than one-fifth of the grade 4 classes sampled for the MLSS, the share of Chichewa-speaking students is between 20 percent and 80 percent, presenting teachers with the difficult task of teaching a multilingual classroom.

### Help with homework

A third of students receive no help at home with school work. The median student spends an average of 10 minutes on homework each day, with 10 percent of students spending more than one hour. Students were most likely to name their mother or an elder sibling as the person most likely to help them with homework; however, 30 percent of students said that they receive no help from family members.

### Range of ages per grade

Within classes, Malawi's students vary widely in age. Over-age and underage enrollments in grade 1, combined with widespread repetition in lower grades, mean that, by grade 4, a typical class contains a wide range of ages. The typical grade 4 student is 11 years old, but sampled grade 4 students in MLSS schools ranged from 7 to 16 years old. Only 59 percent of students in a typical grade 4 class were 10–12 years of age.[7] (For the summary statistics, refer to annex 4A, table 4A.1).

## WHAT MATTERS FOR LEARNING?

### Inequities in outcomes from school-level student population differences

The MLSS findings reveal widespread variation in average student backgrounds between schools—especially between more and less remote schools (box 4.1). We conduct regression analysis to investigate the ways in which differences in school-level student populations affect learning (as shown in chapter 2, annex 2A, table 2A.3, panel a). The findings suggest that demographic and cultural factors, as well as gender, have a decisive impact on a school's performance (refer to table 4.1).

**Household poverty, parental literacy, and support.** Household wealth does not affect a school's performance, but parental literacy and support do. A school's average level of student poverty does not appear to directly affect learning.[8] However, schools where a higher proportion of students have at least one literate

> **BOX 4.1**
>
> ### Inequities in student populations between remote schools and those close to trading centers
>
> Students in remote schools are typically from poorer backgrounds, and are less likely to have literate parents, than students in schools close to trading centers (TCs). Although student characteristics vary significantly within a single school, the Malawi Longitudinal School Survey findings also reveal widespread variation in average student backgrounds between schools—especially between more and less remote schools. Students in remote schools are typically less likely to have a television or bed than students at schools close to a TC, and they are also less likely to have literate parents at home, particularly a literate mother (figure B4.1.1). Students at remote schools spend more time traveling to school than those in schools close to a TC and spend three minutes less time on homework each day.[a]
>
> In our case study schools, at Kamulindeni (relatively close to a trading center), 48 percent of the sampled students have a bed at home, versus 24 percent at Chamkoko (a remote school). In addition, 67 percent of students at Kamulindeni receive help with homework from a family or household member, versus just 56 percent of students at Chamkoko.
>
>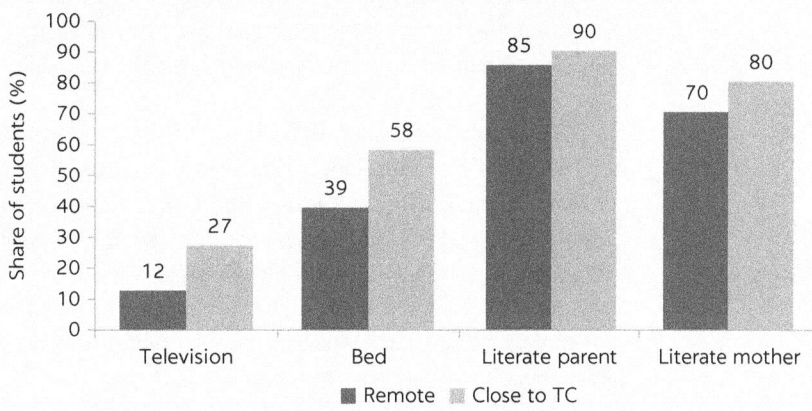
>
> **FIGURE B4.1.1**
>
> **Shares of Malawian students with selected household characteristics in remote schools versus those close to a trading center, 2016**
>
> *Source:* Malawi Longitudinal School Survey baseline (2016) data.
> *Note:* Data include both rural and urban schools. TC = trading center.
>
> a. Remote-school students spent an average 34 minutes traveling to school, versus 31 minutes for students in schools close to a TC. Remote-school students spent an average 19 minutes on homework each day, versus 22 minutes for students in schools close to a TC.

parent at home achieved average test scores that are significantly higher than schools where a lower share do, as did those where a higher share of students report that a relative helps them with their homework.[9] The finding suggests that a supportive environment for learning at home, with support from literate relatives, matters more than wealth for learning achievement.

**Language spoken at home.** Schools with a larger number of minority-language-speaking children have lower average learning outcomes. A 10 percent increase in the share of students at a school who speak Chichewa at home is associated with an increase of 5 points in knowledge scores. This finding suggests that the system is struggling to meet the needs of students who speak Malawi's minority languages.

TABLE 4.1 **Effects on achievement gaps in Malawian schools' student populations, by indicator, 2016**

| | ADJUSTED STUDENT KNOWLEDGE SCORE | |
|---|---|---|
| INDICATOR | BOTTOM QUINTILE OF SCHOOLS | TOP QUINTILE OF SCHOOLS |
| Share of students with at least one literate parent | 498 | 509 |
| Share of students speaking Chichewa at home | **481** | **516** |
| Share of students above median age | **489** | **518** |
| Share of students with pre-primary education | **488** | **518** |
| Share of students in psychological poverty[a] | **510** | **495** |
| Share of students above school's median wealth[b] | 501 | 504 |

Source: Calculations from Malawi Longitudinal School Survey baseline (2016) data.
Note: Table shows the adjusted knowledge scores associated with different school student populations, controlling for a wide range of school, teacher, and student characteristics. **Bold** numbers indicate that the estimated adjusted score gap, statistically, is significantly different from zero ($p = .05$). "Bottom" or "top" quintiles of schools are calculated for the selected indicator.
a. "Psychological poverty" refers to students who demonstrate positive mindsets in two or fewer of four selected indicators.
b. Wealth denotes socioeconomic status, drawn from the number of basic assets available in a student's household.

**Share of underage students and absenteeism rate.** Schools with more students below the median age achieve significantly lower learning outcomes.[10] This finding suggests that the widespread practice of early enrollment is leading students to progress to grade 4 without achieving an appropriate level of learning, exacerbating the problem of classes with a wide range of learning levels. In addition, schools with a greater rate of absenteeism achieve significantly lower learning outcomes.[11]

**Access to pre-primary education.** Schools where more students have a pre-primary education achieve higher learning outcomes. Almost one-third (38 percent) of students in the MLSS sample at baseline reported not having attended even one year of pre-primary education. This lack of provision has important implications for learning. Schools with a higher share of students with a pre-primary background achieve higher learning outcomes: for every increase of 10 percentage points in the share of students with pre-primary education, overall knowledge scores increase by 4 points.

### Student mindset as a driver of learning outcomes

Schools with high proportions of students with positive mindsets have higher learning scores. Evidence from a range of countries suggests that *mindset*—a set of beliefs and attitudes about one's own abilities and qualities—is a key determinant of academic success (Duckworth 2016; Dweck, Walton, and Cohen 2014; Mourshed, Krawitz, and Dorn 2017; Susperreguy et al. 2018).[12]

Preliminary evidence from the MLSS baseline suggests that mindsets are significantly predictive of learning in Malawi. Across all subjects, significantly higher average scores were observed in schools where a higher share of students agreed with statements designed to test positive mindsets, particularly those measuring perseverance and motivation. A 10 percent increase in the share of students agreeing with the statement, "When you start your homework, you tend to finish it," a measure of perseverance, is associated with an increase of 6 points in test scores—more than the increase from having an additional teacher at the school. A similar increase in the share of students who identified with the statement, "Failing in a test frustrates you," a test of motivation, is associated with an increase of 7 points.

> **BOX 4.2**
>
> ### A sample of students' attitudes toward their schools and learning
>
> To further illustrate the Malawian student experience, we interviewed six female grade 4 students from two schools: Mankhamba and Thunga, both in the Thunga zone in Thyolo district. The students interviewed at Mankhamba School ranged from 11 to 14 years of age, whereas all of the students at Thunga Primary School were 14 years old.
>
> Half of the students reported being bullied sometimes for being over the usual age for fourth grade as well as for answering questions in class. One student explained, "They say that I am too old to be in school. I hear this from both boys and girls, especially those from upper classes," and another shared, "They were laughing at me and saying now that I have passed a question that the teacher asked, I should be promoted to the next upper class."
>
> The students we interviewed reported mixed experiences with their teachers and parents. Five out of six students reported that they felt supported by the teachers, although some students reported that teachers shouted at them and suggested that "teachers should make us read more." One student shared, "I wish there was a little more cooperation between our teachers and our parents because that can help us work harder as the parents will be involved in our learning, too." Similarly, two of the six students shared that they do not get any help on school work at home, saying, "I wouldn't have been failing if I got helped at home because I would learn more at home" and "If I got helped [at home], I'd get better grades."
>
> Although mindset is an abstract topic to discuss with students, several students made comments that were illustrative of psychological poverty. One student shared, "I just feel like boys understand things better in my class." After asking her to say more, she explained, "I just fail to understand things that are being taught." Another student shared that she believes she has a lot of self-doubt and that this contributes to her failing in class.

The findings suggest that the opposite of a positive mindset—*psychological poverty*—may be a powerful and hidden factor driving Malawi's large learning inequities. Although these are only preliminary findings, future research will enable more detailed exploration of these dynamics, including exploring the role of socio-emotional learning. Box 4.2 further describes students' attitudes toward their schools and learning.

## CONCLUSIONS: SCHOOL-LEVEL POPULATION DIFFERENCES, PARTICULARLY IN MINDSET, MATTER FOR LEARNING

The MLSS findings show that differences in student characteristics between schools contribute to inequities in learning outcomes. Across the MLSS sample, schools with low levels of parent literacy and support, a large number of minority-language-speaking children, a high proportion of underage students, and a high proportion of students with psychological poverty achieved poorer learning outcomes. Taken together, these findings suggest that certain schools, which have student populations with particular characteristics, face additional challenges in achieving learning. Schools in which these disadvantages are common may require significant extra support to improve learning outcomes.

## ANNEX 4A SUMMARY STATISTICS

TABLE 4A.1 **Summary statistics on student characteristics, 2016**

| CHARACTERISTIC | ALL RURAL SCHOOLS (N = 12,522) | | | | | REMOTE SCHOOLS (n = 2,653) | | SCHOOLS CLOSE TO TC (n = 2,075) | |
|---|---|---|---|---|---|---|---|---|---|
| | MEAN | SD | P10 | P50 | P90 | MEAN | SD | MEAN | SD |
| Student age | 11.45 | 1.65 | 9.00 | 11.00 | 14.00 | 11.67 | 1.59 | 10.97 | 1.64 |
| Student SES index | −0.08 | 1.69 | −1.64 | −0.55 | 2.05 | −0.28 | 1.35 | 0.51 | 2.23 |
| Student is female (%) | 52 | 50 | 0 | 1 | 1 | 52 | 50 | 52 | 50 |
| Student has a physical disability (by observation, %) | 2 | 12 | 0 | 0 | 0 | 2 | 13 | 2 | 13 |
| Student has one or more years of pre-primary education (%) | 62 | 49 | 0 | 1 | 1 | 48 | 50 | 69 | 46 |
| Number of times student has repeated any grade (grades 1–4) | 1.07 | 97 | 0 | 1 | 2 | 1.10 | 96 | 99 | 98 |
| Student has at least one literate parent (%) | 77 | 42 | 0 | 1 | 1 | 77 | 42 | 79 | 41 |
| Student speaks Chichewa at home (%) | 82 | 38 | 0 | 1 | 1 | 78 | 41 | 83 | 38 |
| Student receives help from parents on homework at home (%) | 63 | 48 | 0 | 1 | 1 | 53 | 50 | 67 | 47 |
| Student was absent on any day last week (%) | 31 | 46 | 0 | 0 | 1 | 32 | 47 | 30 | 46 |
| Raw Raven Test score (0–6) | 2.33 | 1.40 | 0 | 2 | 4 | 2.27 | 1.37 | 2.45 | 1.41 |
| Student agrees with "You are interested in talking to new kids in school." (%) | 82 | 39 | 0 | 1 | 1 | 80 | 40 | 82 | 39 |
| Student agrees with "When you start your homework you tend to finish it." (%) | 93 | 25 | 1 | 1 | 1 | 88 | 32 | 96 | 20 |
| Student agrees with "Failing in a test frustrates you." (%) | 85 | 36 | 0 | 1 | 1 | 85 | 36 | 86 | 34 |
| Student agrees with "Teachers or parents often tell you that you are not performing to your potential." (%) | 78 | 41 | 0 | 1 | 1 | 78 | 41 | 78 | 42 |
| Overall knowledge score across subjects | 510 | 117 | 367 | 506 | 661 | 480 | 114 | 527 | 115 |
| English knowledge score | 506 | 127 | 347 | 504 | 676 | 478 | 121 | 527 | 132 |
| Mathematics knowledge score | 510 | 138 | 335 | 514 | 685 | 481 | 136 | 525 | 135 |
| Chichewa knowledge score | 512 | 140 | 337 | 514 | 694 | 481 | 139 | 522 | 135 |

*Source:* Malawi Longitudinal School Survey baseline (2016) data.
*Note:* Sample sizes refer to students. Parental literacy is defined as having at least one literate parent. See table 1A.1 for details of included schools and chapter 2 for definitions of "remote" and "close to TC" schools. P10 = 10th percentile; P50 = 50th percentile; P90 = 90th percentile; SD = standard deviation.

## NOTES

1. The baseline survey carried out extensive interviews with more than 13,000 randomly selected students from grade 4, including questions on their family and home life, journey to school, opinions about school, teachers, and attitudes and aspirations for the future. For summary statistics of student characteristics, refer to annex 4A, table 4A.1.
2. As throughout this report, "typical" refers to the median. Unless otherwise stated, all specified statistics are for rural schools only.

3. In predominantly agricultural economies, monetary income is a poor measure of wealth; instead, the MLSS collects information on the number of basic assets in a student's home.
4. We define a socioeconomic status index drawn from the number of basic assets available in a student's household. The list includes bed(s), bicycle(s), chickens, refrigerator, goats, mobile phone, motorcycle or scooter, pigs, radio, sheep, stove, tractor or truck, and television.
5. To assess parental literacy, we asked students whether they had ever seen their mother or father reading the Bible, a book, or a newspaper at home.
6. The Ministry of Education (then the Ministry of Education, Science and Technology) introduced a new language policy in 1996 (IN/2/14) that recommended use of mother tongues in grades 1–4, followed by instruction in English. However, the National Education Act of 2013 stipulates English as the language of instruction in all grades, leading to some incoherence in terms of official policy regardless of realities on the ground. In practice, Chichewa is the most commonly used language in lower grades. The other most frequently used language is Kacci, a common language in southern areas.
7. The selection of students to interview for the MLSS was done from a single stream (class), enabling us to identify the extent of variation in students' backgrounds and learning outcomes within the same classroom.
8. We identify the share of students at a school who are above the median of the entire student population for socioeconomic status. A 10 percent increase in this share is not associated with a significant change in average learning outcomes.
9. Every 10 percent increase in the share of students with at least one literate parent is associated with an increase in test scores of 5 points. A 10 percent increase in the share of students reporting that a relative helps them with their homework is associated with a score increase of 4 points.
10. For every additional 10 percent of sampled students from a school who are above the median age for sampled grade 4 students nationwide, a school's average knowledge scores increase by 9 points.
11. For every additional 10 percent of sampled students from a school who were absent from school in the week preceding the interview, a school's average knowledge scores decrease by 5 points.
12. Mindsets relevant to academic performance include motivation, a "growth mindset" (the extent to which students feel that their ability to perform stems from effort rather than being predetermined), and perseverance or "grit." These mindsets were assessed by asking whether students agreed or disagreed that certain statements described them—statements such as "Failing a test frustrates you" and "When you start your homework you tend to finish it." In addition, mindsets relating to social motivation and negative feedback were measured using the statements, "You are interested in talking to new kids in school" and "Teachers or parents often tell you that I am not performing to your potential."

## REFERENCES

Duckworth, A. 2016. *Grit: The Power of Passion and Perseverance*. New York: Scribner.

Dweck, C., G. Walton, and G. Cohen. 2014. "Academic Tenacity: Mindsets and Skills that Promote Long-Term Learning." White paper prepared for the Bill & Melinda Gates Foundation, Seattle. https://ed.stanford.edu/sites/default/files/manual/dweck-walton-cohen-2014.pdf.

Mourshed, M., M. Krawitz, and E. Dorn. 2017. "How to Improve Student Educational Outcomes: New Insights from Data Analytics." Discussion paper, McKinsey & Company, New York.

Susperreguy, M. I., P. E. Davis-Kean, K. Duckworth, and M. Chen. 2018. "Self-Concept Predicts Academic Achievement across Levels of the Achievement Distribution: Domain Specificity for Math and Reading." *Child Development* 89 (6): 2196–214.

# 5 Focus on Girls' Learning

## KEY POINTS

The Malawi Longitudinal School Survey (MLSS) baseline data reveal that although school-level student population differences contribute to disparities, differences between individual students are the main drivers of inequity in educational outcomes. Gender is the single most impactful personal characteristic for student-level outcomes, with girls significantly disadvantaged compared with boys as early as grade 4.

Awareness of gender disparities by school leaders, inclusion of women in leadership roles, and community support can all contribute to closing the gender gap. Promising reforms, such as the learner mentors program and efforts to build a larger cohort of female leaders, suggest a way forward.

## STUDENT-LEVEL INEQUITIES: THE MAIN SOURCE OF OUTCOME DISPARITIES

Although significant inequities exist between schools, the differences between individual students, even at the same school, account for most of the variation in learning outcomes in Malawi (refer to box 5.1). Despite the wide range of variation in school conditions, 73 percent of the variation observed in learning outcomes was found between individual grade 4 students within a school (refer to table 5.1). This is a greater level of within-school variation than in several other African countries.[1]

## BOX 5.1

### Influence of personal characteristics on student-level outcomes

Chapter 4 explored the influence of student *population* factors on school-level learning outcomes. Our analysis of personal characteristics and students' *individual* learning outcomes reveals similar findings:

- *Students without literate parents underperform.* Students with at least one literate parent achieve knowledge scores 6 points higher than those without, controlling for other factors.
- *Students with poor mindsets underperform.* Students who agree that "When you start your homework you tend to finish it"—a measure of perseverance, or "grit"—achieve scores 19 points higher than those who disagree. Other statements such as "Failing in a test frustrates you" are also associated with higher learning outcomes.
- *Older students underperform relative to their peers.* Although at the *school* level, a higher share of underage students is associated with lower learning outcomes, at the *individual* level, students *above* median age achieve overall knowledge scores 8 points lower than those below median age. The impact persists even when controlling for whether a student has repeated a grade (which is itself also significantly associated with lower learning). This finding suggests that students above median age underperform primarily in classes where they are one of a small number of older students.

*Note:* Findings are estimated using a hierarchical linear regression model and controlled for school characteristics, teacher populations, and student populations as well as students' innate intelligence (refer to chapter 2, annex 2A, table 2A.3, panel d).

TABLE 5.1 **Decomposition of variance in test scores**

| DECOMPOSITION DIMENSION | PROPORTION OF TOTAL VARIANCE | | | |
| --- | --- | --- | --- | --- |
| | ALL (1) | ENGLISH (2) | MATH (3) | CHICHEWA (4) |
| Between divisions (Strata) | 0.01 | 0.01 | 0.01 | 0.02 |
| Within divisions, between schools | 0.26 | 0.19 | 0.20 | 0.21 |
| Within schools, between students | 0.73 | 0.81 | 0.79 | 0.77 |
| Total variation | 0.60 | 0.71 | 0.84 | 0.86 |

*Source:* Calculations from Malawi Longitudinal School Survey baseline (2016) data.
*Note:* The table presents a three-level variance decomposition analysis to test the share of variation in learning outcomes that occurs between divisions, between schools, and between individual students.

## FEMALE STUDENTS ARE LEFT BEHIND IN MALAWI'S PRIMARY SCHOOLS

At grade 4, girls have already fallen behind in learning in Malawi's primary schools. Although several individual characteristics emerged as influential for learning at grade 4 (as noted in box 5.1), analysis of the MLSS finds that gender is the single most impactful personal characteristic. Girls underperform in lower-primary grades, achieving scores 19 points lower than boys, equivalent to about four months' less learning (refer to figure 5.1). This disadvantage persists even when controlling for parental literacy, mindsets, and other factors, suggesting a role for less tangible factors such as teacher behavior and school cultures.

### FIGURE 5.1
**Distribution of knowledge scores, by gender, 2016**

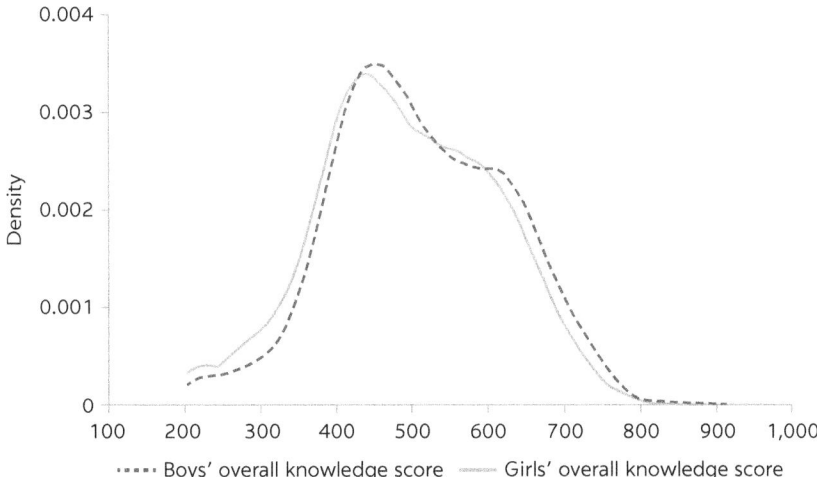

*Source:* Malawi Longitudinal School Survey baseline (2016) data, World Bank.
*Note:* Scores are at student level. For more information on knowledge score construction, refer to box I.3 and the online technical appendix (https://openknowledge.worldbank.org/handle/10986/40948).

### TABLE 5.2 Contrast in knowledge scores, by student characteristic, 2016

| CHARACTERISTIC | OVERALL KNOWLEDGE SCORE | |
| --- | --- | --- |
| Gender | Girls, 494 | Boys, 513 |
| Repetition of grade | Repeaters, 506 | Nonrepeaters, 512 |
| Absenteeism | Absent last week, 494 | Present last week, 507 |
| Grade-appropriate age | Over-age (>14 years), 499 | Appropriate age (11 years), 507 |
| Parental literacy | Illiterate parents, 499 | Literate parents, 504 |
| Language | Minority-language-speaking, 499 | Chichewa-speaking, 505 |

*Source:* Malawi Longitudinal School Survey baseline (2016) data, World Bank.
*Note:* The table compares the predicted value of the overall knowledge score for contrasting groups of students. These predicted values are estimated from hierarchical linear regression model after controlling for student, teacher, and school characteristics. For more information on knowledge score construction, refer to box I.3 and the online technical appendix (https://openknowledge.worldbank.org/handle/10986/40948).

The impact of gender persists in all subjects but is strongest in mathematics and weakest in Chichewa.[2] The impact of gender is larger than that of age, parental literacy, home language, and other factors (refer to table 5.2).

Dropout rates are higher for girls in upper grades. The MLSS shows that, in lower primary, girls drop out at rates similar to or even lower than those for boys. In upper primary, however, this pattern is reversed, and by grade 7 girls drop out at a significantly higher rate than boys (refer to figure 5.2, panel a). As a result, school demographics shift considerably: the share of girls in a typical school declines from 51 percent in grade 1 to 46 percent in grade 8. Ultimately, girls are 6 percent less likely than boys to enter the Primary School Leaving Certificate Examinations (PSLCE) and 13 percent less likely than boys to pass (refer to figure 5.2, panel b).

FIGURE 5.2
**Primary school dropout rates and PSLCE outcomes, by gender**

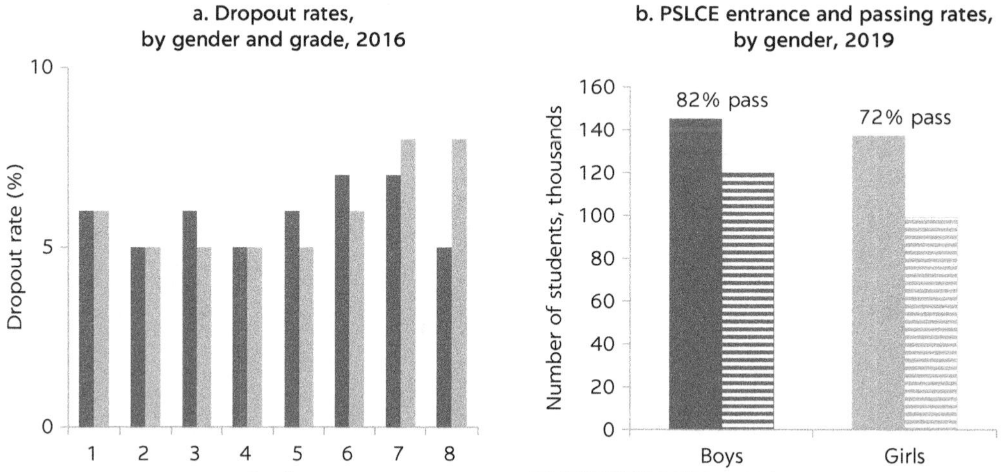

a. Dropout rates, by gender and grade, 2016

b. PSLCE entrance and passing rates, by gender, 2019

|  | Boys | Girls |
|---|---|---|
| Entered | 145,158 | 137,270 |
| Passed | 119,714 | 99,042 |

82% pass (Boys); 72% pass (Girls)

■ Boys entered  ≡ Boys passed
▨ Girls entered  ≡ Girls passed

*Sources:* Malawi Longitudinal School Survey baseline (2016) data, World Bank; Malawi National Examinations Board.
*Note:* PSLCE = Primary School Leaving Certificate Examinations.

## WHAT MATTERS FOR GIRLS' LEARNING?

### Quantitative analysis

To estimate whether school-level factors affect girls' learning differently, we run a series of multivariate regressions. We estimate both whether school-level factors affect girls' learning (refer to annex 5A, table 5A.1) and whether the impact on girls differs from that on boys (refer to annex 5A, table 5A.2).[3] We find that several factors appear to show different dynamics between girls and boys.

Female school leaders benefit all students, particularly girls. In addition to the lack of female teachers in a large share of schools,[4] there is a severe lack of women in senior teaching positions in Malawi. Although 45 percent of teachers are women, only about 14 percent of headteachers are women.

Controlling for other factors, the presence of a woman in a leadership position[5] at a school is associated with a large increase in test scores—particularly for female students. Girls at schools with a female leader achieved scores 21–26 points higher in MLSS learning assessments (refer to the unconditional models in annex 5A, table 5A.1), with the largest impact in English (24.1 points). For boys, the effect was similar but smaller, with test score gains of 21–25 points.

The results from the multilevel modeling with cross-level interactions show a similar finding (refer to annex 5A, table 5A.2). The finding suggests that building the cohort of female school leaders may increase both the overall quality and the equity of the school system by benefiting all students.

Girls develop less resilience than boys to large class sizes. We identified schools where the typical class size in grade 1 was more than 100 students. Strikingly, grade 4 students in these schools, regardless of gender, achieve *higher* knowledge scores than those in schools with less extreme class sizes in grade 1—the opposite of the expected effect. This finding likely reflects some selection effect—that is, the students who reach grade 4 in these schools are those with the most resilience and capacity for learning in challenging environments.

However, these resilience and selection effects are stronger for boys than for girls. Grade 4 boys in schools with grade 1 class sizes above 100 achieve scores 19–27 points higher than those in other schools, whereas for girls the difference is 14–17 points (see full models in annex 5A, table 5A.2). This finding suggests that, even with these selection effects, girls do not achieve the same level of resilience as boys. The result is that the gender gap in learning is significantly larger in schools with class sizes above 100 in grade 1.

### Qualitative analysis

Although the MLSS collects data on a wide range of school conditions and practices, unobserved factors may also explain the persistent gender differences in learning. To identify other, previously unobserved factors, we first conducted a residual analysis[6] of multivariate regressions to identify schools where girls perform comparatively better or worse than would be predicted from the observed covariates model.[7]

We then identified schools with the largest unexplained variance by gender, using average scores across grades. We identified schools where girls underperform the predicted scores by 40 points or more and boys overperform by the same amount (13 schools). In addition, we identified schools where girls overperform predictions by 40 points or more and boys underperform by the same amount (21 schools).

We then conducted qualitative interviews with the headteachers of a sample of each type of school to learn about their attitudes, and those of their communities, toward girls' learning as well as actions taken by the schools to address gender inequities in learning.[8] The interviews reveal several key trends, described in the following paragraphs.

Schools where girls underperform are typically unaware of the problem. At all of the schools with underperforming girls, headteachers stated that, in general, girls perform either better than or at the same level as boys. By contrast, of the surveyed schools with overperforming girls, headteachers were as likely to say that girls generally underperformed as that they overperformed.[9] This finding suggests that lack of awareness of girls' underperformance is a key factor in its persistence.

Schools where girls underperform are more likely to describe community views about girls' education as negative. Although headteachers of both types of schools reported favorable views of their own toward girls' education, headteachers of schools where girls generally underperform were substantially more likely to report that their community held negative views.[10] This finding may partially explain why these schools were also less likely to mobilize support from the community to help female learners, as explained in the following paragraphs.

Schools with better-performing girls provide substantially more support to girls. The survey confirmed that schools where girls achieve higher learning outcomes are typically those where more action is taken to support girls. Headteachers of both types of schools reported providing counseling by Mother Groups and female teachers, menstrual health management materials, girls' clubs, and one-on-one support from head teachers to struggling female pupils. However, headteachers of schools where girls perform better additionally reported providing rewards to high-performing girls, making improvements to sanitary facilities such as building change rooms, providing uniforms using the headteachers' own personal funds, and mobilizing female role models to visit schools.

Schools where girls perform better also typically mobilize more support from communities. In schools where girls underperform, headteachers reported that communities provide limited support specifically to girls' learning, primarily through the formulation of bylaws to require parents to ensure girls' attendance. By contrast, in schools where girls perform better, headteachers reported a much wider range of community support strategies specifically targeting female learners, including fundraising, community construction of sanitary facilities, procurement and manufacturing of menstrual health management materials, and frequent visits by the Mother Group to schools.

Schools where girls perform better are more likely to have a woman in a leadership position. Only 1 of the 21 schools surveyed across both categories had a female headteacher, reflecting the severe lack of women in that position in Malawi. However, 60 percent of schools with better-performing girls had a female deputy headteacher versus just 25 percent of schools with underperforming girls. This finding reinforces the analysis that schools with females in a leadership position help girls achieve higher learning outcomes.

## CONCLUSIONS: CONTRIBUTIONS OF INDIVIDUAL STUDENT CHARACTERISTICS, PARTICULARLY GENDER, TO INEQUITIES IN LEARNING OUTCOMES

Student-level characteristics, particularly gender, substantially contribute to inequities in learning outcomes. Analysis of the MLSS data reveals that most variation in learning outcomes is between students within a school: older students achieve significantly lower outcomes, as do students who lack at least one literate parent, students who did not receive pre-primary education, and students who lack a positive mindset. These inequities between students persist even when controlling for school conditions, remoteness, and teacher characteristics. However, the most significant student characteristic for learning outcomes is gender.

Analyses of MLSS data reveal policy insights for targeting gender equity. Quantitative analysis suggests that increasing the number of female school leaders and reducing class sizes would raise the learning outcomes of girls. However, qualitative analysis suggests that, in addition to these hard investments, a wide range of low-cost strategies—including engagement of communities to support girls as learners—can have positive impacts on girls' learning and can help address gender disparities while longer-term reforms are made.[11]

New reforms, informed by the MLSS data, have begun to tackle divergence in girls' learning outcomes in lower grades. Between 2019 and 2022, learner mentors—female secondary-school students (originally known as "learner guides") who provide pastoral and academic support to girls—were introduced in 675 Malawian schools by the Campaign for Female Education (CAMFED) through the Strengthening Malawi's Education System project supported by the United Kingdom's Foreign, Commonwealth and Development Office. This scheme is now being scaled up under the Malawi Education Reform Program (MERP) to more than 2,000 schools that have a severe lack of female teachers and leaders, with a greater emphasis on supporting girls in lower primary. In addition, MERP supports district-level action to improve the distribution of female teachers between schools, as well as gender-disaggregated reporting on student test scores to schools to raise awareness of gender inequities in learning.

## ANNEX 5A REGRESSION ANALYSES

TABLE 5A.1 **Impact of school-level factors on female students' school-level learning**

| | GIRLS' KNOWLEDGE SCORES AT SCHOOL LEVEL | | | | | |
|---|---|---|---|---|---|---|
| | SCHOOL HAS A WOMAN IN A LEADERSHIP POSITION | | GRADE 1 CLASS SIZE EXCEEDS 100 (ENROLLMENT) | | SHARE OF STUDENTS WITH 1+ YEARS OF PRE-PRIMARY EDUCATION (PER 10 PP)[a] | |
| | UNCONDITIONAL MODEL | FULL MODEL | UNCONDITIONAL MODEL | FULL MODEL | UNCONDITIONAL MODEL | FULL MODEL |
| **a. Overall score** | | | | | | |
| School characteristic | 23.8*** | 14.2*** | 28.4*** | 14.1** | 8.0*** | 4.0*** |
| | (6.2) | (5.5) | (6.8) | (6.9) | (0.9) | (1.0) |
| Constant | 479.6*** | 273.8*** | 473.0*** | 295.9*** | 439.3*** | 366.9*** |
| | (4.8) | (101.2) | (5.8) | (102.0) | (7.0) | (98.3) |
| Rural schools (n) | 503 | 487 | 502 | 486 | 491 | 475 |
| $r^2$ | 0.03 | 0.41 | 0.03 | 0.41 | 0.14 | 0.44 |
| Adjusted_$r^2$ | 0.03 | 0.35 | 0.03 | 0.35 | 0.14 | 0.38 |
| **b. English score** | | | | | | |
| School characteristic | 24.1*** | 13.3** | 22.0*** | 12.5* | 7.1*** | 3.2*** |
| | (6.0) | (5.5) | (6.8) | (7.0) | (0.9) | (1.0) |
| Constant | 477.0*** | 303.1*** | 474.9*** | 323.2*** | 443.4*** | 397.4*** |
| | (4.6) | (95.1) | (5.9) | (95.3) | (6.7) | (86.9) |
| Rural schools (n) | 503 | 487 | 502 | 486 | 491 | 475 |
| $r^2$ | 0.03 | 0.38 | 0.02 | 0.38 | 0.12 | 0.41 |
| Adjusted_$r^2$ | 0.03 | 0.32 | 0.02 | 0.32 | 0.11 | 0.35 |
| **c. Mathematics score** | | | | | | |
| School characteristic | 21.1*** | 13.0** | 27.3*** | 13.4* | 8.5*** | 5.1*** |
| | (6.7) | (5.9) | (7.3) | (7.8) | (1.0) | (1.1) |
| Constant | 478.8*** | 262.0** | 471.4*** | 282.4** | 433.6*** | 342.1*** |
| | (5.2) | (108.9) | (6.1) | (109.9) | (7.7) | (109.3) |
| Rural schools (n) | 503 | 487 | 502 | 486 | 491 | 475 |
| $r^2$ | 0.02 | 0.36 | 0.03 | 0.36 | 0.14 | 0.40 |
| Adjusted $r^2$ | 0.02 | 0.30 | 0.03 | 0.30 | 0.13 | 0.33 |
| **d. Chichewa score** | | | | | | |
| School characteristic | 26.2*** | 16.3*** | 35.8*** | 16.4** | 8.5*** | 3.8*** |
| | (7.0) | (6.3) | (7.5) | (7.4) | (1.0) | (1.1) |
| Constant | 483.2*** | 256.3** | 472.6*** | 282.2** | 441.0*** | 361.3*** |
| | (5.3) | (116.8) | (6.3) | (117.8) | (7.8) | (116.0) |
| Rural schools (n) | 503 | 487 | 502 | 486 | 491 | 475 |
| $r^2$ | 0.03 | 0.40 | 0.04 | 0.40 | 0.12 | 0.43 |
| Adjusted_$r^2$ | 0.03 | 0.34 | 0.04 | 0.34 | 0.12 | 0.37 |

*Source:* World Bank calculations from Malawi Longitudinal School Survey baseline (2016) data.
*Note:* Coefficients were estimated with ordinary least squares regressions at the school level with the aggregated female score subject as the dependent variable. Each panel reports the results for a separate subject. Estimates under the columns labeled "Unconditional models" come from regressions with the dependent variable adjusted by student gender, a school characteristic, and an interaction term for both terms. Results reported in columns labeled "Full models" include adjustments by aggregated student and teacher characteristics as well as school characteristics. Robust standard errors are shown in parentheses.
a. Coefficient represents the change in dependent variable per change of 10 percentage points (pp) in the share of students with 1+ years of pre-primary education.
*$p$ <0.10  **$p$ <0.05  ***$p$ <0.01

TABLE 5A.2 **Differential impact on learning of student gender, school-level factors, and cross-level interactions**

| | SCHOOL HAS A WOMAN IN A LEADERSHIP POSITION | | GRADE 1 CLASS SIZE EXCEEDS 100 (ENROLLMENT) | | SHARE OF STUDENTS WITH 1+ YEARS OF PRE-PRIMARY EDUCATION (PER 10 PP)[a] | |
|---|---|---|---|---|---|---|
| | UNCONDITIONAL MODEL | FULL MODEL | UNCONDITIONAL MODEL | FULL MODEL | UNCONDITIONAL MODEL | FULL MODEL |
| *a. Overall score* | | | | | | |
| Student is female = 1 | −18.9*** (2.7) | −20.6*** (2.7) | −11.4*** (3.3) | −14.1*** (3.4) | −21.4*** (4.2) | −21.2*** (4.2) |
| School characteristic | 18.7*** (5.9) | 13.2*** (5.1) | 28.2*** (7.0) | 22.6*** (6.5) | 8.2*** (0.9) | 4.4*** (1.0) |
| Cross-level interaction | 0.5 (3.6) | 2.3 (3.6) | −10.2** (4.0) | −7.3* (4.0) | 0.4 (0.6) | 0.3 (0.6) |
| Constant | 475.7*** (6.4) | 222.0*** (83.4) | 471.5*** (6.5) | 240.2*** (83.1) | 434.8*** (7.7) | 317.3*** (82.9) |
| *b. English score* | | | | | | |
| Student is female = 1 | −20.6*** (3.1) | −22.8*** (3.1) | −13.5*** (3.8) | −16.7*** (3.9) | −21.7*** (4.7) | −22.1*** (4.8) |
| School characteristic | 18.5*** (5.7) | 10.9** (5.0) | 24.2*** (6.8) | 19.0*** (6.4) | 7.2*** (0.9) | 3.3*** (0.9) |
| Cross-level interaction | 2.2 (4.1) | 4.5 (4.1) | −8.2* (4.5) | −5.0 (4.6) | 0.4 (0.6) | 0.3 (0.6) |
| Constant | 483.7*** (6.1) | 244.3*** (80.2) | 481.0*** (6.2) | 259.2*** (79.8) | 448.3*** (7.5) | 331.7*** (80.4) |
| *c. Mathematics score* | | | | | | |
| Student is female = 1 | −24.3*** (3.3) | −24.7*** (3.3) | −14.7*** (4.1) | −16.0*** (4.2) | −28.5*** (5.1) | −27.6*** (5.2) |
| School characteristic | 18.5*** (6.5) | 14.1** (5.6) | 33.6*** (7.6) | 27.1*** (7.1) | 8.7*** (1.0) | 5.2*** (1.0) |
| Cross-level Interaction | −1.3 (4.4) | −0.3 (4.5) | −14.6*** (4.8) | −12.6** (4.9) | 0.5 (0.7) | 0.4 (0.7) |
| Constant | 483.1*** (6.9) | 198.2** (90.4) | 476.4*** (7.0) | 215.7** (89.7) | 439.3*** (8.3) | 296.0*** (89.5) |
| *d. Chichewa score* | | | | | | |
| Student is female = 1 | −11.9*** (3.3) | −14.3*** (3.4) | −5.9 (4.1) | −9.6** (4.2) | −14.0*** (5.2) | −13.9*** (5.2) |
| School characteristic | 19.0*** (6.6) | 14.6** (5.8) | 26.7*** (7.8) | 21.6*** (7.4) | 8.7*** (1.0) | 4.8*** (1.1) |
| Cross-level interaction | 0.7 (4.5) | 2.6 (4.5) | −7.7 (4.9) | −4.4 (4.9) | 0.4 (0.7) | 0.2 (0.7) |
| Constant | 460.2*** (7.0) | 220.2** (93.2) | 457.1*** (7.2) | 242.5*** (93.1) | 416.4*** (8.6) | 321.0*** (92.9) |
| *Observations* | | | | | | |
| Schools (L2) | 504 | 488 | 503 | 487 | 494 | 478 |
| Students (L1) | 12,504 | 12,071 | 12,479 | 12,046 | 12,254 | 11,821 |
| *Controls* | | | | | | |
| Students' characteristics (aggregated at L2) | No | Yes | No | Yes | No | Yes |
| Teachers' characteristics (aggregated at L2) | No | Yes | No | Yes | No | Yes |

*continued*

**TABLE 5A.2,** *continued*

| | SCHOOL HAS A WOMAN IN A LEADERSHIP POSITION | | GRADE 1 CLASS SIZE EXCEEDS 100 (ENROLLMENT) | | SHARE OF STUDENTS WITH 1+ YEARS OF PRE-PRIMARY EDUCATION (PER 10 PP)[a] | |
|---|---|---|---|---|---|---|
| | UNCONDITIONAL MODEL | FULL MODEL | UNCONDITIONAL MODEL | FULL MODEL | UNCONDITIONAL MODEL | FULL MODEL |
| Schools' characteristics (L2) | No | Yes | No | Yes | No | Yes |
| Students' characteristics (L1) | No | Yes | No | Yes | No | Yes |
| Division fixed effects | Yes | Yes | Yes | Yes | Yes | Yes |

*Source:* World Bank calculations from Malawi Longitudinal School Survey baseline (2016) data.
*Note:* Coefficients correspond to a set of hierarchical linear modeling (HLM) regressions with student-level scores in each tested subject as the dependent variable. Results reported in columns labeled "Unconditional models" are for regressions including adjustments by student gender, school characteristic, and a cross-level interaction of both terms. Results reported in columns labeled "Full models" add, to the previous specification, adjustments by students' characteristics at level 1 (L1), school characteristics measured at level 2 (L2), and teachers' and students' characteristics aggregated at L2. HLM regressions are fitted via maximum likelihood with an unstructured variance-covariance matrix for random effects. Standard errors are reported in parentheses.
a. Coefficient represents the change in dependent variable per change of 10 percentage points (pp) in the share of students with 1+ years of pre-primary education.
*$p<0.10$   **$p<0.05$   ***$p<0.01$

# NOTES

1. In the Southern and Eastern African Consortium for Monitoring Education Quality (SACMEQ) III (2007) and Program for the Analysis of Educational Systems of CONFEMEN (PASEC) 2014 assessments, the level of within-school variation in Malawi was greater than that in 19 of 26 countries for reading and 17 of 26 countries for mathematics (Bashir et al. 2018).
2. Girls achieved scores 25 points lower than boys in mathematics, 13 points lower in Chichewa, and 20 points lower in English.
3. Two models are specified: the first is an unconditional model to estimate the magnitude of the association between a school-level factor on girls' learning, and the second (full model) is conditional on a set of school-level controls (refer to annex 5A, table 5A.1). We used girls' scores in each subject (averaged at school level) as the dependent variable. In addition, we conducted a multilevel regression analysis of students' scores nested within schools to estimate the presence of cross-level interactions, if a school-level characteristic has a different impact if the student is male or female (refer to annex 5A, table 5A.2).
4. Female teachers are disproportionately clustered in schools close to trading centers and in lower grades. As a result, the average remote school has 163 female students to every female teacher in upper primary, and only 13 percent of upper-primary teachers in such schools are female.
5. To capture the wide range of leadership positions that women may occupy, we assigned a dummy variable to schools with a woman in at least one of the following positions: headteacher, deputy headteacher, section head (infant, junior or senior), School Management Committee chair or vice chair, and parent-teacher association chair or vice chair.
6. The residual analysis used the same multilevel regression analysis described in the previous chapters, including both school and student characteristics.
7. We derived estimates of the scores predicted by the model for male and female students at each school in English, mathematics, and Chichewa.
8. In total, interviews were conducted in 21 schools. Each interview was conducted by phone (because of the COVID-19 pandemic) and lasted 45–60 minutes.
9. Of 9 schools with underperforming girls, 4 reported girls generally performing better than boys, and 5 reported girls and boys generally performing at the same level. By contrast, of 12 schools with overperforming girls, 5 reported girls generally performing worse than boys, 5 reported girls generally performing better, and 2 reported both genders generally performing at about the same level.

10. Headteachers were asked whether they and their communities would agree with the statements, "Girls are as capable as boys of learning, or more capable" and "Girls should prioritize preparing for careers over preparing for motherhood and family." Headteachers were also asked whether their community would agree with a third statement: "It's the responsibility of the entire community to ensure girls learn." Headteachers of schools where girls generally underperform were substantially more likely to say that communities would generally disagree with each of these three statements.
11. Evidence from Tanzania and Zimbabwe suggests that learner mentors have had positive impacts on girls' retention and learning outcomes in lower-secondary school (CAMFED 2020).

## REFERENCES

Bashir, S., M. Lockheed, E. Ninan, and J. Tan. 2018. *Facing Forward: Schooling for Learning in Africa*. Washington, DC: World Bank.

CAMFED (Campaign for Female Education). 2020. "Evidence of Impact of CAMFED's Programme, Focused on the Learner Guide." Unpublished document, CAMFED, Cambridge, UK.

# 6 The Effect of Multiple Disadvantages on Student Achievement

## KEY POINTS

Lacking high-quality school-level data, reforms to date have been broadly targeted. Using the high-resolution picture that the Malawi Longitudinal School Survey (MLSS) data provide of school conditions, and the analyses shared in this paper, we develop a Disadvantage Index (DI) to capture key school characteristics with a demonstrated impact on learning. As expected, a school's DI is highly predictive of its learning outcomes, demonstrating the ways in which multiple disadvantages have negative effects on learning. The DI is thus a tool for policy makers to identify the neediest schools and target support to address inequities between schools.

## INTRODUCING THE DISADVANTAGE INDEX

The DI is designed to obtain a clearer picture of the ways in which multiple dimensions of disadvantage interact. It identifies five key factors that reflect school conditions, staffing, and student populations, which the preceding analysis reveals to have a negative effect on student progression and learning outcomes. These factors include remoteness, extremely large class sizes, a lack of female leaders, severe shortages of student learning materials, and a low share of students with pre-primary education (figure 6.1 and box 6.1). These disadvantage conditions are each met by 16–28 percent of schools (as shown in annex 6A, table 6A.1). The resulting index assigns a DI of 0–5 to schools based on the number of disadvantage conditions they are experiencing.

Multiple disadvantages tend to exist in a single school. If disadvantages were randomly distributed between schools, we might expect most schools to have a DI of zero or 1. In fact, 22 percent of schools have a DI of 2, and 7 percent a DI of 3 or more. At a national scale, this finding suggests that more than 1,900 schools across Malawi have two or more disadvantages. A school

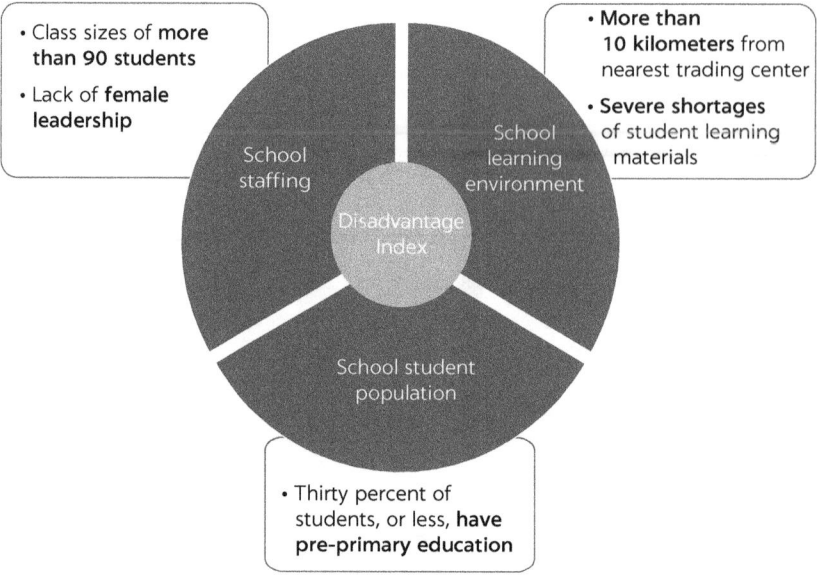

FIGURE 6.1

**School conditions included in the Disadvantage Index**

- Class sizes of **more than 90 students**
- Lack of **female leadership**
- More than **10 kilometers** from nearest trading center
- **Severe shortages** of student learning materials
- Thirty percent of students, or less, **have pre-primary education**

Source: World Bank.

---

**BOX 6.1**

### The Disadvantage Index

The Disadvantage Index includes the following five disadvantages:[a]

1. School is more than 10 kilometers from the nearest trading center.
2. School has no women among the headteacher; deputy headteacher; infant, junior, and senior section heads; School Management Committee chair and vice chair; or Parent-Teacher Association chair and vice chair.
3. School has both a pupil-teacher ratio and a pupil-classroom ratio above 90 to 1.
4. Less than 30 percent of students have one or more year of pre-primary education.
5. School meets three or four shortage conditions for student learning materials (SLM): pupil-desk ratio of 5 to 1 or higher; pupil-textbook ratio of 4 to 1 or higher; less than 80 percent of students with pens and notebooks; less than 25 percent of students with a uniform.

a. Note that these are the same indicators as in the SLM Index in chapter 2 (annex 2A and table 2A.3, panel c) but with higher thresholds in some cases. These disadvantages are strongly correlated with students' achievement. Results are consistent for English, mathematics, and Chichewa.

---

in this category might be far from the trading center, have a severe shortage of senior teachers, and have a low share of students with a pre-primary background. Approximately 71 percent of the variation in DI is between schools within a single district.[1]

As expected, school DIs are highest in remote schools and lowest in schools close to trading centers. Among schools close to trading centers, only 13 percent of schools have two or more disadvantages, whereas 61 percent of remote schools are in this category. In the example of our case study schools, Kamulindeni, the better-performing of the two in terms of average learning outcomes, has a DI of 1, and Chamkoko has a DI of 4.[2]

FIGURE 6.2

**Average knowledge scores at primary schools, by number of disadvantages, 2016**

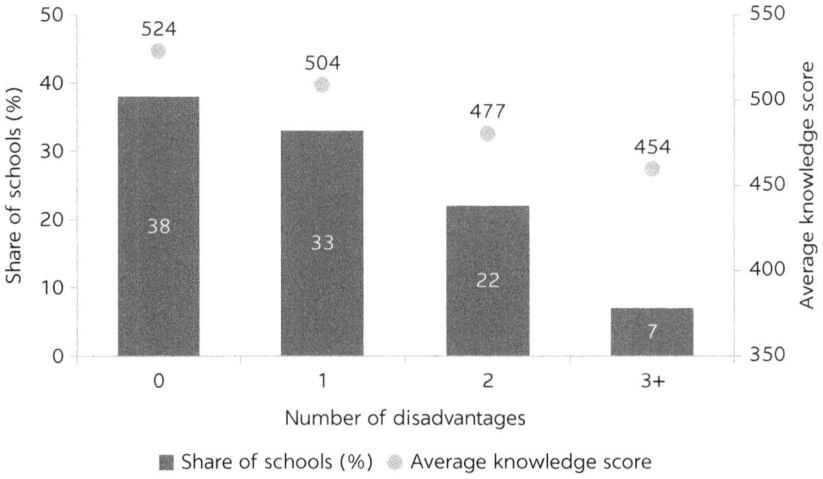

Source: Malawi Longitudinal School Survey baseline (2016) data, World Bank.

## PROFOUND IMPACT OF MULTIPLE DISADVANTAGES ON LEARNING OUTCOMES

A regression analysis estimates the impact of each additional disadvantage on school average learning outcomes (refer to annex 6A, table 6A.2). It shows that, across subjects, each additional school-level disadvantage reduces average learning scores by approximately 20–30 points. The addition of two disadvantages reduces a school's average learning outcomes by about 50 points, equivalent to about one year's learning. This finding means that students in more than one-quarter of schools face an additional learning challenge of at least one year compared with those in the 38 percent of schools with zero disadvantages. Figure 6.2 presents the distribution of schools by disadvantage and average knowledge scores across subjects for each DI level.

The findings suggest that within Malawi's school system exist at least two highly distinct systems. One system is made up of schools facing few disadvantages, achieving average learning outcomes above the median. The other comprises schools facing multiple disadvantages, achieving learning outcomes well below the median. Simply being born in a village with a school that has three or more disadvantages can reduce a student's learning level by grade 4 by the equivalent of a year's learning.

## HOW TARGETED INVESTMENTS IN THE NEEDIEST SCHOOLS CAN IMPROVE LEARNING

This section estimates the impact of targeted learning environment improvements on learning outcomes in schools facing severe constraints. Specifically, we model the impact of two key investments supported by the forthcoming Malawi Education Reform Program (MERP) project: construction of low-cost classrooms and appointment of additional teachers in lower primary.

Under MERP, communities will construct approximately 10,900 low-cost lower-primary classrooms in schools with lower-primary pupil-classroom ratios (PCRs) above 90 to 1. Furthermore, about 4,000 auxiliary teachers have been appointed to teach lower grades in schools whose lower-primary pupil-teacher ratios (PTRs) exceed 90 to 1, substantially reducing the share of schools with severe overcrowding in lower primary.[3]

To fully estimate the association between improved learning environments and learning outcomes, this simulation presents a scenario in which the levels of construction and hiring are adequate to eliminate severe overcrowding in lower primary. In the simulation, over four years, schools are assigned an adequate number of classrooms and teachers to reduce PCRs and pupil-qualified teacher ratios (PqTRs) in lower primary to below 90 to 1, up to a maximum of four classrooms and teachers per year. In the final year, the maximum rates are raised to eight classrooms and teachers to ensure elimination of PCRs above 90 to 1.[4]

The results illustrate the sheer scale of the investment required to produce even minimally adequate learning environments in all of Malawi's schools, with construction of 17,200 classrooms and hiring and retention of 7,555 teachers (including the MERP investments) required to eliminate severe overcrowding.[5] Even using the low-cost classroom model introduced under MERP, the estimated cost is US$150 million over five years.[6]

We then estimate the impact of the reductions in class sizes obtained through these investments on learning outcomes. To take a conservative approach, we base our estimated correlations from evidence on the impacts of PqTR reduction specifically.[7] Inequity in PqTRs is highly correlated with remoteness, making PqTR reduction a useful initial estimation of the impacts of targeted investment in disadvantaged schools. Future analyses will simulate the impacts of addressing other school-level disadvantages on learning.

We create two estimates of the correlation between PqTRs and learning to demonstrate the range of possible impacts on learning outcomes. For our lower-impact projections, we estimate the correlation based on regression analysis of the MLSS data (in chapter 2, annex 2A, table 2A.3, panel c) showing the effect on grade 4 learning outcomes of PTRs below 90 to 1.

For our higher-impact projections, we estimate the correlation between reduced PTR and learning identified in a large-scale experimental evaluation of PTR reduction through appointment of contract teachers in rural India (Muralidharan and Sundararaman 2013).[8]

In both cases, we compare the improvement in learning outcomes with a counterfactual "business as usual" model of hiring of teachers in the next few years, based on historical trends.[9]

Annex 6A, table 6A.3 presents the findings. Panel a of the table presents findings for the PqTR and scores impacts on all public primary schools.[10] Panel b of the table presents findings for schools with either PCR or PqTR above 90 to 1 in lower primary at the beginning of the simulation. Figure 6.3 illustrates the impact on scores in each of four scenarios for schools with severe overcrowding at baseline. For this population of schools, the effect of reducing PqTRs is large, with scores improving by 23.6 points more than in the counterfactual after four years, equivalent to several months' additional learning.

FIGURE 6.3

**Estimated knowledge scores in overcrowded schools where PqTR is reduced**

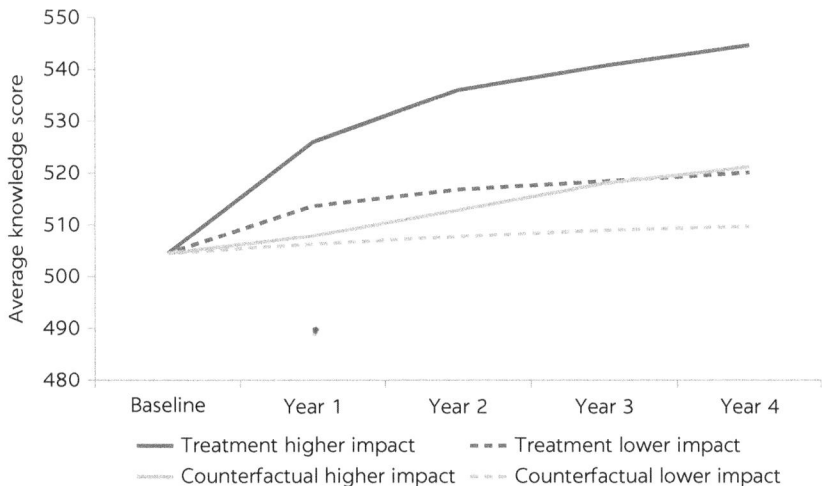

*Source:* Calculations from Malawi Longitudinal School Survey baseline (2016) data, World Bank.
*Note:* Figure depicts the knowledge score impact of the pupil-qualified teacher ratio (PqTR) reduction in schools with severe overcrowding (defined as a PqTR or a pupil-classroom ratio exceeding 90 to 1 in grades 1–4).

This preliminary analysis suggests that substantial gains in learning can be achieved through targeted investments in learning environments in the neediest schools. Investing in additional teachers and targeting them to schools with PqTRs above 90 to 1 are projected to increase average learning outcomes by the equivalent of several months' learning compared with a less targeted approach. MERP provides support to significant levels of classroom construction and hiring of auxiliary teachers at schools with severe overcrowding in lower primary, but additional investment will be required to unlock these learning benefits in all schools.

## CONCLUSIONS: RAISING LEARNING OUTCOMES BY TARGETING RESOURCES TO DISADVANTAGED SCHOOLS

Multiple school-level disadvantages related to conditions, staffing, and student populations combine to severely affect students' learning. Simply being born in a village with a school that has three or more disadvantages can reduce a student's learning level by grade 4 by the equivalent of a year's learning. However, preliminary analysis suggests that targeted investment in the neediest schools can address these disadvantages. Targeting additional teachers to reduce all school PTRs below 90 to 1 could increase the overall national level of achievement in grade 4 by the equivalent of several months' learning relative to current levels of hiring and targeting.

## ANNEX 6A STATISTICAL AND REGRESSION TABLES

TABLE 6A.1 **Distribution of school disadvantage conditions**

| DISADVANTAGE CONDITION | DEFINITION | SHARE OF RURAL SCHOOLS (%) |
|---|---|---|
| Remoteness | School is more than 10 kilometers from nearest trading center. | 16 |
| Severe shortage of SLM | School meets three or four shortage conditions for SLM.[a] | 23 |
| Lack of female leadership | No females among headteacher; deputy headteacher; infant, junior, and senior section heads; SMC chair and vice chair; or PTA chair and vice chair. | 28 |
| Low access to pre-primary education | Share of students in the school with 1+ years of pre-primary education is below 30 percent. | 16 |
| Class size | PCR and PTR are above 90 to 1. | 17 |

*Source:* Malawi Longitudinal School Survey baseline (2016) data, World Bank.
*Note:* Disadvantage conditions are identified through multivariate analysis. PCR = pupil-classroom ratio; PTA = parent-teacher association; PTR = pupil-teacher ratio; SMC = School Management Committee.
a. Student learning materials (SLM) shortage conditions include the following: pupil-desk ratio of 5 to 1 or higher; pupil-textbook ratio of 4 to 1 or higher; less than 80 percent of students with pens and notebooks; less than 25 percent of students with a uniform. These are the same indicators as in the SLM Index in chapter 2 (annex 2A, table 2A.3, panel c) but with higher thresholds in some cases.

TABLE 6A.2 **Regression estimates on key outcome indicators, by Disadvantage Index**
*Robust OLS regressions*

| CHARACTERISTIC | OVERALL SCORES | ENGLISH SCORES | MATH SCORES | CHICHEWA SCORES | TRANSITION RATE[a] | OUTPUT EFFICIENCY[b] | GRADE 4 SURVIVAL[c] | GRADE 8 SURVIVAL[c] | DROPOUT RATE[d] | REPETITION RATE[e] |
|---|---|---|---|---|---|---|---|---|---|---|
| Intercept | 524.74*** | 519.79*** | 525.93*** | 528.49*** | 0.86*** | 0.49*** | 0.49*** | 0.28*** | 0.06*** | 0.21*** |
|  | (3.76) | (3.67) | (3.98) | (4.18) | (0.01) | (0.01) | (0.01) | (0.01) | (0.00) | (0.01) |
| Disadvantage Index[f] | −22.70*** | −20.87*** | −23.26*** | −23.96*** | −0.02** | −0.02** | 0.01 | −0.03*** | −0.00 | −0.01* |
|  | (3.02) | (2.76) | (3.34) | (3.33) | (0.01) | (0.01) | (0.01) | (0.01) | (0.00) | (0.01) |
| School size[g] | Yes | Yes | Yes | Yes | Yes | Yes | Yes | Yes | Yes | Yes |
| Division absorbed FE | Yes | Yes | Yes | Yes | Yes | Yes | Yes | Yes | Yes | Yes |
| Schools | 502 | 502 | 502 | 502 | 478 | 479 | 494 | 388 | 502 | 502 |
| $r^2$ | 0.166 | 0.149 | 0.143 | 0.186 | 0.040 | 0.229 | 0.092 | 0.084 | 0.063 | 0.035 |
| Adjusted $r^2$ | 0.155 | 0.137 | 0.131 | 0.175 | 0.026 | 0.218 | 0.079 | 0.067 | 0.050 | 0.022 |

*Source:* Calculations from Malawi Longitudinal School Survey baseline (2016) data.
*Note:* Scores are averages at school level. FE = fixed effects; OLS = ordinary least squares.
a. Transition rate is the percentage of students enrolled in the last grade of lower primary education who transition to the first grade of upper primary education.
b. Output efficiency is a proxy measure of internal school efficiency. It is estimated as the total enrollment in upper primary divided by the total enrollment in lower primary.
c. Survival rates are the percentage of students enrolled in grade 1 who are expected to reach a certain grade, regardless of repetition.
d. Dropout rate is the share of enrolled students who drop out each year, averaged across grades 1–8.
e. Repetition rate is the share of repeaters of enrollment averaged between grades 1 and 8.
f. Disadvantage Index is a summative scale ranging from 0 to 5; because of the sparsity of cases with scores of 4 and 5, these were grouped and recoded into score 3.
g. School size is measured by enrollment, specified in the regression model as centered around the mean.
*$p < 0.05$  **$p < 0.01$  ***$p < 0.001$

TABLE 6A.3 **Knowledge score impact of PqTR reduction**

| YEAR | PQTR | | OVERALL KNOWLEDGE SCORES | | | |
|---|---|---|---|---|---|---|
| | | | TREATMENT | | COUNTERFACTUAL | |
| | TREATMENT | COUNTERFACTUAL | LOWER IMPACT | HIGHER IMPACT | LOWER IMPACT | HIGHER IMPACT |
| a. All schools (N = 5,770)[a] | | | | | | |
| Baseline | 85.8 | 85.8 | 500.5 | 500.5 | 500.5 | 500.5 |
| Year 1 | 70.8 | 79.1 | 506.7 | 514.9 | 501.7 | 502.7 |
| Year 2 | 71.2 | 74.4 | 509.1 | 521.7 | 502.7 | 506.0 |
| Year 3 | 72.3 | 70.7 | 510.3 | 524.9 | 503.5 | 509.5 |
| Year 4 | 73.4 | 67.5 | 511.7 | 527.6 | 504.0 | 511.7 |
| b. Schools with severe overcrowding at baseline (n = 3,817)[b] | | | | | | |
| Baseline | 100.5 | 100.5 | 504.6 | 504.6 | 504.6 | 504.6 |
| Year 1 | 77.3 | 91.9 | 513.8 | 526.2 | 506.4 | 508.0 |
| Year 2 | 77.3 | 85.4 | 517.0 | 536.3 | 507.9 | 513.0 |
| Year 3 | 78.5 | 80.2 | 518.6 | 541.0 | 509.1 | 518.2 |
| Year 4 | 79.6 | 75.5 | 520.3 | 545.0 | 509.9 | 521.4 |

*Source:* Calculations from Malawi Longitudinal School Survey (MLSS) baseline (2016) data, World Bank.
*Note:* Lower bound is simulated using a statistically significant constant effect size of 13.25 score points associated with schools whose pupil-qualified teacher ratio (PqTR) is less than 90 to 1, calculated using MLSS baseline 2016. Upper bound is simulated using the Muralidharan and Sundararaman (2013) effect size in which a one-unit decrease in pupil-teacher ratio is associated with an increase in standardized test scores of 0.014 standard deviation, equivalent to approximately 1.4 score points on the MLSS scale.
a. All schools in Malawi with nonzero enrollment in all of grades 1–4.
b. "Schools with severe overcrowding" have a pupil-classroom ratio exceeding 90 to 1 or a PqTR exceeding 90 to 1 in the grade 1–4 baseline year (before the simulated interventions).

## NOTES

1. Of the 88 percent of the total variance attributed to higher DI levels, 71 percent corresponds to schools within districts within divisions (strata), of which 14 percent corresponds to the variance between districts within a division, and 3 percent of the variation is attributed to the differences between divisions.
2. Kamulindeni's disadvantage is a low share of students with a pre-primary education. Chamkoko's disadvantages are remoteness, severe shortages of student learning materials, a lack of female leaders, and a low share of students with a pre-primary education.
3. World Bank (2021) estimates that following these investments, by 2025, about 30 percent of schools will still have PCRs above 90 in these grades (down from 61 percent in 2019), and a similar share will still have PTRs above 90 in these grades (down from 38 percent in 2019). These restrictions are a result of financial limitations, with investments in classrooms and teachers accounting for US$86 million of the total US$150 million World Bank and Global Partnership for Education financing for the MERP program.
4. The simulation assumes an enrollment growth rate of 2.3 percent per year, evenly applied across schools.
5. A small number (less than 1 percent) of schools remain above the threshold ratio of 90 to 1 (25 schools for PCR and 28 for PqTR).
6. Even these large investments would be smaller than the targets set by the government of Malawi in the National Education Sector Investment Plan, which calls for construction of 44,000 low-cost classrooms by 2030 along with the reduction of the national PTR to 60 to 1, requiring an estimated 30,000 additional teachers by 2030.
7. Note, however, that anecdotal evidence suggests that additional teachers are of limited use in schools with severe classroom shortages. Schools that gain an extra teacher without an available classroom are likely to pair the new teacher with an existing teacher to share a large class rather than breaking the class into two, with no resulting reduction in class sizes.

8. Muralidharan and Sundararaman (2013) estimate that a one-unit decrease in PTR is associated with an increase in standardized test scores of 0.014 standard deviation, equivalent to approximately 1.4 points on the MLSS knowledge score.
9. Specifically, we model an increase in the national stock of teachers of 3,000 per year, allocated randomly to schools with PTRs above 60 to 1. This roughly approximates the historical trend in Malawi's teacher allocations, whereby districts have been required to target schools with PTRs above 60 to 1 but have received little more specific guidance (Asim et al. 2019).
10. We limit the analysis to all schools with nonzero enrollment in all of grades 1–4.

## REFERENCES

Asim, S., J. Chimombo, D. Chugunov, and R. Gera. 2019. "Moving Teachers to Malawi's Remote Communities: A Data-Driven Approach to Teacher Deployment." *International Journal of Educational Development* 65: 26–43.

Muralidharan, K., and V. Sundararaman. 2013. "Contract Teachers: Experimental Evidence from India." Working Paper 19440, National Bureau of Economic Research, Cambridge, MA.

World Bank. 2021. "International Development Association Project Appraisal Document on a Proposed Credit in the Amount of SSR 13.2 Million (US$18.7 Million Equivalent) and a Proposed Grant in the Amount of SDR 52.5 Million (US$74.8 Million Equivalent) and a Grant in the Amount of US$56.5 Million from the Global Partnership for Education to the Republic of Malawi for a Malawi Education Reform Program Project (MERP)." Report no. PAD4212, World Bank, Washington, DC.

# Conclusion
## THE CHALLENGE AND OPPORTUNITY OF LONGITUDINAL EDUCATION DATA

### SUMMARY OF FINDINGS FROM BASELINE DATA

The findings from the Malawi Longitudinal School Survey (MLSS) baseline confirm that Malawi's education system is struggling to deliver learning to its students. Students who do advance to grade 4 struggle even with items aligned with the grade 1–2 curricula. Only 5 percent of students correctly answered more than 50 percent of items aligned with the grade 3–4 curricula in English. About 15 percent of students achieved a score of zero on grade 1 items in each subject, meaning that they have progressed to grade 4 having learned almost nothing. The COVID-19 pandemic, and the associated seven-month closure of schools, has exacerbated these poor outcomes, leading to several months' loss of learning.[1]

Poor learning environments exacerbate low learning outcomes, particularly in remote schools. The typical school lacks basic teaching and learning materials, has infrastructure in severe need of repair, and has extremely large class sizes in lower grades. These problems are most severe in schools in remote areas, which are also more likely to lack an adequate number of teachers, particularly senior and female teachers.

Within schools, there is also significant inequity in learning outcomes between students. Girls achieve lower average test scores than boys as early as grade 4, suggesting disparities in learning beginning at the very start of the schooling cycle. Students without literate parents, who speak minority languages at home, and who lack a pre-primary education also achieve lower learning outcomes on average. Initial evidence suggests that students experiencing psychological poverty also achieve lower learning outcomes.

### DATA-DRIVEN REFORMS, INVESTMENTS, AND ANALYSES

Since 2016, promising recent interventions and reforms have begun to address key constraints to learning. The Malawi Education Sector Improvement Project (MESIP), implemented from 2016 to 2021, introduced some promising pilot interventions to raise learning outcomes, including enhanced grants to schools, community engagement using information and communication technology, and support to improved school leadership (refer to box I.1 in the introduction to this book). Forthcoming impact evaluations, supported by the MLSS midline and endline data, will provide rigorous experimental evidence of the impact of these interventions on learning.

Other programs—including the National Reading Programme implemented since 2016 with the support of the United States Agency for International Development and the United Kingdom's Foreign, Commonwealth and Development Office (FCDO), as well as the Strengthening Malawi's Education System project implemented from 2018 with the support of the FCDO—have made promising investments at a larger scale to support improved learning by raising the skills of teachers and supporting girls.

The MLSS has supported new, data-driven approaches to more equitable investment in the education system in Malawi. Informed by the MLSS baseline findings, the National Education Sector Investment Plan 2020–30 included equity-based targets for pupil-classroom ratio and pupil-teacher ratio for the first time in a Malawi National Education Sector Plan, specifically committing the government to address conditions in the most overcrowded schools. The new Malawi Education Reform Program (MERP) targets resources to schools with specific shortages, for the first time providing targeted support to individual schools based on need (as also discussed in box I.1).

Forthcoming analyses, using data from the MLSS midline and endline data, will explore the impacts of recent reforms and of the COVID-19 pandemic on learning. The MLSS longitudinal data enable precise measurement of the changes in school conditions and practices as a result of MESIP and other reforms—and the impact of those changes on student outcomes. The data will also provide additional analysis of the COVID-19 pandemic's impact, through both school closures and changes in students' learning trajectories following their return to school. In addition, forthcoming analyses will further explore the sources of and potential responses to gender disparities in learning in lower grades.

## OUTLOOK FOR LONGITUDINAL DATA-DRIVEN POLICY MAKING IN LOW-INCOME COUNTRIES

The MLSS and associated analyses represent a novel approach to data-driven policy making, based on precise, high-quality longitudinal data. Although many countries' education management information systems include information on education inputs, these systems tend to lack data on student learning. As a result, inputs often become the focus of political agendas (World Bank 2018, 2021).

Several countries, such as India and Ethiopia, have conducted surveys of student learning, enabling analysis of student learning over time and informing the evaluation of interventions.[2] With longitudinal data on school characteristics *and* student learning, education policy making can transition from an input orientation to a learning outcomes orientation, powering systems change and improvements in learning.

Several challenges remain for implementing a longitudinal, data-driven approach to policy making in Malawi and in other low-income countries. First, although donors increasingly demand data-driven evidence to inform investments that increase quality learning, they also tend to invest in data collection efforts that are tied to specific projects. As a result, there are mismatches in software, hardware, and questionnaires between projects (Bashir et al. 2018). Second, hiring consulting firms for data collection and analysis in stand-alone projects can result in poor-quality data and inconsistent sample designs, harming the quality of final data outputs (World Bank 2013, 2016).

Development partners can use financing more efficiently, produce better data outputs, and analyze learning trajectories by coordinating longitudinal data collection *across* projects funded by different partners. Although resource intensive, such an approach enables donors to evaluate the impact of their investments on outcomes of interest. Embedding longitudinal data collection within large investment projects in Sub-Saharan Africa can help to move the needle on hard-to-change education outcomes. Forthcoming analysis will demonstrate how this was the case for MESIP, as noted in the introduction to this book (box I.2).

A second challenge is the need to produce timely education data to iteratively improve interventions. Previous data collection efforts, such as the World Bank's Service Delivery Indicators, provided information about the state of education service delivery but were not designed to provide real-time feedback on interventions. The MLSS baseline, midline, and endline surveys were linked to the MESIP project cycle, enabling changes in intervention designs when necessary. As a result, the MLSS has provided critical data for evaluating MESIP's success while also informing and supporting the investments included in MERP. Moving forward, coordination between longitudinal survey timelines and project timelines can maximize the lessons gained from investments.

## NOTES

1. The Government of Malawi closed all public schools because of COVID-19 between March and October 2020 and again in January–February 2021. An analysis of the learning impacts is forthcoming (Asim, Bashir, and Casley Gera, forthcoming).
2. In India, the Annual Status of Education Report provides yearly estimates of children's enrollment and learning levels for every district and state in India (ASER Centre 2023). In Ethiopia, the Young Lives School Surveys of 2016–17 measured children's learning and progression over a single school year (Rossiter, Azubuike, and Rolleston 2021).

## REFERENCES

ASER Centre. 2023. "Annual Status of Education Report 2023: Beyond Basics." ASER Centre, New Delhi. https://asercentre.org/aser-2023-beyond-basics/.

Asim, S., S. Bashir, and R. Casley Gera. Forthcoming. "Learning Loss as a Result of COVID-19: Dynamic Analysis from Malawi." Policy Research Working Paper, World Bank, Washington, DC.

Bashir, S., M. Lockheed, E. Ninan, and J. Tan. 2018. *Facing Forward: Schooling for Learning in Africa*. Washington, DC: World Bank.

Rossiter, J., O. B. Azubuike, and C. Rolleston. 2017. *Young Lives School Surveys 2016-17: Ethiopia Country Report*. Oxford, UK: Young Lives.

World Bank. 2013. "Project Appraisal Document on a Proposed Credit in the Amount of SDR 259.6 Million (US$400 Million Equivalent) to the Islamic Republic of Pakistan for a Second Sindh Education Sector Project." Report No. 74552-PK, World Bank, Washington, DC.

World Bank. 2016. "International Development Association Project Appraisal Document on a Proposed Grant in the Amount of US$44.9 Million to the Republic of Malawi for a Malawi Education Sector Improvement Project (MESIP)." Report No. PAD1515, World Bank, Washington, DC.

World Bank. 2018. *World Development Report 2018: Learning to Realize Education's Promise.* Washington, DC: World Bank.

World Bank. 2021. *World Development Report 2021: Data for Better Lives.* Washington, DC: World Bank.

# APPENDIX A

# Data and Methodology

## MALAWI LONGITUDINAL SCHOOL SURVEY

### Objectives and methodology

The Malawi Longitudinal School Survey (MLSS) attempts to anchor education policy choices and sector dialogue firmly in school-level data, which not only complements the existing education management information systems but also, for the first time, provides robust estimates of students' learning at the school level. It collects extensive data on schools, classrooms, teachers, grade 4 students, community members, and parents. The baseline round was conducted in two phases from May to November 2016 in a representative sample of 559 primary schools (509 in rural areas) in all districts of Malawi.

During the baseline round, the survey contained 10 core components:

- Facilities observation
- Lesson observation
- Headteacher interviews
- Student interviews
- Student learning assessment
- Teacher interviews
- Teacher knowledge assessment
- School Management Committee member interviews
- Parent-teacher association executive committee member interviews
- Mother Group member interviews.

Data collection was carried out by an independent research firm contracted by the World Bank in partnership with the Ministry of Education. Data collection was conducted through unannounced visits to schools to obtain a true picture of everyday conditions and practices. Additional announced visits were conducted, as well as telephone calls, to complete data collection that was not possible to complete during the unannounced visit.

Within each school, the respondent sample included 25 randomly selected grade 4 students; 10 teachers selected randomly and for balance across gender and lower/upper grades; the headteacher; and 3 active, office-holding members of each of the School Management Committee, parent-teacher association executive committee, and Mother Group.

### The added value of the MLSS

Malawi has been the subject of numerous national and international surveys of learning in recent years, including the United States Agency for International Development Early Grade Reading Assessment (EGRA) and Early Grade Math Assessment (EGMA) as well as multiple rounds of the Southern and Eastern African Consortium for Monitoring Education Quality (SACMEQ). Evidence from cross-country analyses suggests that a significant proportion of students who fall behind in learning in early grades never progress beyond a very low level of learning (Crouch and Rolleston 2015).

The MLSS complements the learning assessments carried out in grade 2 by EGRA and EGMA and in grade 6 by SACMEQ with assessments of a random sample of grade 4 students. The MLSS thus provides an important check on the learning levels of students on the cusp of entering upper-primary grades. Whereas international learning assessments are frequently aligned with the competencies expected for the assessed grade, the MLSS assessments contain items aligned with the curricula from all grades 1 through 6. This approach enables students who are lagging behind to complete some tasks, providing a nuanced picture of differential learning levels. The MLSS includes learning assessments in English, mathematics, and Chichewa, providing a broad picture of differential learning levels across subjects similar to the World Bank's Service Delivery Indicators survey in comparable countries.

The MLSS also extends the scope of previous assessments carried out in Malawi in key areas to reflect emerging ideas about the drivers of learning. Evidence from a range of low- and middle-income countries suggests that teaching practices—including time spent teaching, proper introduction and summary of lessons, and setting and marking of homework—have a significant impact on learning (Bashir et al. 2018; Murnane and Ganimian 2014). The MLSS conducts observations of grade 4 English and mathematics lessons, carried out in the classes sampled for learning assessments, enabling robust analysis of the impact of teaching practices on learning in Malawi.[1]

In addition, a growing body of research suggests that students' attitudes and beliefs have a significant impact on learning performance (Mourshed, Kravitz, and Dorn 2017). The MLSS includes a series of questions designed to assess students' attitudes to school and beliefs about their abilities, enabling rigorous analysis of the impact of these factors on learning.

For more on the MLSS, including sampling, instrument design, and indicator construction, refer to the online technical appendix (https://openknowledge.worldbank.org/handle/10986/40948).

## ANALYTICAL APPROACHES

### Hierarchical linear model

Modeling the impact of school-level and individual student-level characteristics on student-level learning outcomes requires a strategy that allows us to disentangle the impact of specific school-level from student-level characteristics. One common approach—to conduct the analysis at the lowest level (student level) and ignore the possible presence of between-group variation (for example, between schools)—violates the independence assumption between errors as school-level characteristics; hence, the relationship between higher- and lower-level characteristics on student outcomes cannot be identified. Alternatively, we can conduct a higher-level analysis aggregating all the student-level characteristics at the school level, but the individual variation is sacrificed, and the interpretation of results at the student level is lost.

A hierarchical linear model (HLM) is pertinent for our analysis because it recognizes the nested structure of the data whereby students are grouped into classrooms, which in turn are nested within schools. This modeling enables simultaneous consideration of *school-level* variation (between schools) and *student-level* variation (between students within schools) and provides estimates of the impact of characteristics at all levels on student-level learning outcomes.

Our modeling strategy starts by setting up a simple null random intercept model that allows us to decompose and attribute the variation in student-level test performance to two levels: students and schools. The model becomes more complex as we sequentially add, as explanatory variables, the characteristics of the higher-level units (schools) and then the lower-level units (students). At each stage it is possible to estimate how much of the variation share is reduced and what percentage is explained by the introduction of a new set of predictors. We finalize with a full model that includes all identified predictors.

To assess the model stability due to changes in entry order of predictors, we run separate models to identify whether randomly shuffling the position of a predictor in the full model affects the estimated coefficients or its statistical significance. None of the predictors in our model is affected by a change in its entry order.

Our main HLM (as shown in chapter 2, annex 2A, table 2A.3) includes school-, teacher-, and student-level characteristics but does not include indicators based on lesson observations, which are presented separately in chapter 3, annex 3A, table 3A.3. The sampling method for lesson observations—in which the largest grade 4 class is selected for observation over two lessons—does not produce a sample that is adequately representative of all lessons at the school.

## Disadvantage Index

The Disadvantage Index (DI) is a measure that identifies a smaller set of attributes (reflecting school conditions, staffing, and student populations), which the HLM and other regression analyses reveal to have a negative effect on student survival[2] and learning outcomes. The components of the index are proxy measures derived from some predictors identified in the full HLM regression specification.

We started with several characteristics, which then were aggregated at the school level. We decanted for indicators at the school level to reduce measurement errors due to aggregation from lower levels. A subset of indicators with lower correlation between them was identified and then dichotomized using threshold values so each indicator would retain approximately 15–30 percent of the schools.[3]

The resulting index is calculated as a summative indicator built from the aggregation of each of the five components identified. The index assigns a DI "score" of 0–5 to schools based on the number of disadvantage conditions they are experiencing.

All items have equal weights to each of the components because each one captures a similar amount of the school-level variance, between 2.4 percent and 3.2 percent.

## NOTES

1. The lesson observation tool is a simplified version of the Stallings tool, adapted from that used by the Service Delivery Indicators.
2. The survival rate of a certain grade is the percentage of students enrolled in grade 1 who are expected to reach a certain grade, regardless of repetition.
3. The actual incidence in final DI ranges from 16 percent to 28 percent of schools for each condition. Refer to chapter 5, annex 5A, table 5A.1.

## REFERENCES

Bashir, S., M. Lockheed, E. Ninan, and J. Tan. 2018. *Facing Forward: Schooling for Learning in Africa*. Washington, DC: World Bank.

Crouch, L., and C. Rolleston. 2015. "Raising the Floor on Learning Levels: Equitable Improvement Starts with the Tail." RISE Insights note, Research on Improving Systems of Education, Washington, DC.

Moursched, M., M. Krawitz, and E. Dorn. 2017. "How to Improve Student Educational Outcomes: New Insights from Data Analytics." Discussion paper, McKinsey & Company, New York.

Murnane, R., and A. Ganimian. 2014. "Improving Educational Outcomes in Developing Countries: Lessons From Rigorous Evaluations." *Review of Educational Research* 86 (3): 719–55.

www.ingramcontent.com/pod-product-compliance
Lightning Source LLC
Chambersburg PA
CBHW060517300426
44112CB00017B/2702